C000112190

IMAGES OF ENGLAND

THEATRES & CINEMAS OF THE WAKEFIELD DISTRICT

MUTINY ON THE BOUNTY

ABC WAKEFIELD

SUNDAY 17th NOVEMBER
For 7 Days only

T.F. Ltd. London, N.1

IMAGES OF ENGLAND

THEATRES & CINEMAS OF THE WAKEFIELD DISTRICT

KATE TAYLOR

TEMPUS

Frontispiece: Mutiny on the Bounty (1935) was one of the first films shown at the Regal, Wakefield.

First published 2007

Tempus Publishing Limited
The Mill, Brimscombe Port,
Stroud, Gloucestershire, GL5 2QG
www.tempus-publishing.com

© Kate Taylor, 2007

The right of Kate Taylor to be identified as the Author
of this work has been asserted in accordance with the
Copyrights, Designs and Patents Act 1988.

All rights reserved. No part of this book may be reprinted
or reproduced or utilised in any form or by any electronic,
mechanical or other means, now known or hereafter invented,
including photocopying and recording, or in any information
storage or retrieval system, without the permission in writing
from the Publishers.

British Library Cataloguing in Publication Data.
A catalogue record for this book is available from the British Library.

ISBN 978 0 7524 4281 3

Typesetting and origination by Tempus Publishing Limited.
Printed in Great Britain.

Contents

Acknowledgments

Many organisations and individuals have helped me in the preparation of this book. I am grateful for permission to use material which is the copyright of the Cinema Organ Society, the Cinema Theatre Association, the Dean and Chapter of York Minster, the *Pontefract and Castleford Express*, the Tony Moss Collection, the *Wakefield Express*, Wakefield Metropolitan District Council Cultural Services, Archaeological Services at West Yorkshire Archaeology Service, and Yorkshire Weekly Newspapers. Ed Dennison Associates have been most generous in providing me with photographs from their archaeological surveys.

I am also grateful to the following individuals for information, illustrations, for many of which they hold the copyright, and their patience!

John Brightman, Mrs Carroll, Brian Clayton, the Revd Ian Critchley, Michael Crossland, Don Crossley, Jean Dodd, Joan Egan, Les Ellis, Norman Ellis, John Ellison, Dr John Gatecliff, John Goodchild, Mervyn Gould, Joe Haigh, Margaret Hall, Rosemary Hall, Roy Hampson, Bob Hayhurst, Rick Hayward, John Hodgkins, Brian Hornsey, Joan Howe, Gary Hunt, Dennis Hurst, Donald Issatt, Valerie Kemp, Derek Lines, Keith Lister, David Lumb, Tony Lumb, Cllr H. Mills, Ruth Nettleton, Richard Norman, Bryan Owen, Ian Oxley, Clive Polden, Harry Rigby, Richard Van Riel, Marian Roberts, David Scriven, Deborah Scriven, Ken Smith, Teresa Smith, Dr Terry Spencer, Frank Thompson, Joan Wilkinson, June Wilkinson, Clifford Shaw, Peter Wood, and Peter Wrenn.

Kate Taylor

Introduction

Wakefield Metropolitan District, the area covered by this book, was formed in 1974 under the national scheme of local government reorganisation. Wakefield had, until then, been a county borough and, since medieval times, had served as the county town of the West Riding of Yorkshire. In 1974 the new District took in towns and villages of very varied character including Wakefield itself, Castleford, Featherstone, Hemsworth, Horbury, Knottingley, Normanton, Pontefract, Ossett, South Elmsall, South Kirkby and the surrounding smaller places. Much of this area had developed rapidly in the nineteenth century as industrialisation took place. In Castleford, for example, the principal industries included glass making and pottery. Wakefield's economy grew with the corn trade, the textile industry and engineering. Ossett prospered from mungo and shoddy. Once transport, either by inland waterways or rail, made it economical, coal mining became pervasive. Fitzwilliam owes its very name to colliery proprietors.

The first purpose-built theatres in the District came in the latter part of the eighteenth century in the socially-important Pontefract and Wakefield where a middle class and gentry were ready to provide an audience. Pontefract, which is an ancient borough, had many inhabitants from the professional class. Wakefield, by the late eighteenth century, had its professional men and its merchant princes, prospering from the trade in both raw wool and finished cloth. Close to both towns were country houses whose owners were also to be found at the theatre.

Companies of travelling players were drawn to Wakefield at the time of the races, which were held in September. The area's first purpose-built theatre was erected in 1776, by a private individual, for one of the most celebrated of these companies, that of Tate Wilkinson, the actor manager who controlled the York Circuit. The theatre at Pontefract, built by a group of subscribers a dozen years later, was again intended for Wilkinson's company.

Whilst only Wakefield, Castleford, and Pontefract ever had purpose-built theatres, public rooms, in particular Assembly Rooms, might be licensed for theatrical performances elsewhere. Such rooms were established in Wakefield in the eighteenth century and in Castleford, Normanton, Featherstone and Pontefract in the nineteenth century.

As people had both a little more leisure time and a little spare money, theatrical entertainment came to small towns and villages, especially from the latter part of the nineteenth century, in the form of portable theatres. The records of the West Riding County Council, as the licensing authority from 1889, show the extent of these and reveal, too, that a number were managed by women. George H. Cooper in *Fifty Years' Journalistic Experience*, has left an account of one: 'The theatre was a substantial wooden pavilion, with an improvised gallery of the open-seating type; and how eagerly we saved our weekly threepence for the Saturday evening performances, to revel in exciting periods of such old plays as 'Maria Martin', 'The Dumb Man of Manchester', or 'Uncle Tom's Cabin'. Every now and then the management announced "a fashionable night, under the patronage of the Freemason brethren" (the owner was himself a member of the Craft), and a Shakespearian piece was presented as proof of the company's versatility and adaptability'.

Moving pictures came to the Wakefield area, as to many other parts of the country, from 1896. They were shown at fairgrounds, in Assembly Rooms and other halls (including swimming baths) and as part of the programme of variety theatres.

How far films were shown commercially in public houses before 1910 it is impossible to say. However the 1909 Cinema Act required the licensing annually of all premises where films were shown on a commercial basis and West Riding County Council records show that between 1910 and 1912 more than a dozen hostelries in the Wakefield District obtained licences. In 1912 members of the County Council's General Purposes Committee appear to have decided that the venues were inappropriate and no further licences were granted.

From 1910 at least, existing halls, such as the saloon of the Corn Exchange at Wakefield and the Co-operative Society hall at Horbury, were converted for the regular showing of films. Dual-purpose buildings, intended for both live entertainment and films, were built between 1911 and 1912 in Featherstone, Hemsworth and Moorthorpe. By 1912, however, purpose-built picture houses were to be found in many parts of the district.

Initially many cinemas were built as independent enterprises by people who often had other business interests as well. Gradually, however, many originally independent cinemas were acquired by the proprietors of circuits. The Star chain, which became extensive and survived until the 1970s was actually founded in Castleford. Walter Eckart, then in business as a toy importer, who founded the chain, leased the Star Cinema there in 1931. Whilst Star did not build cinemas itself, Eckart's company went on to acquire cinemas well beyond the Wakefield District, but others in the area covered by this book include the Empire, the Majestic and the Grand – all at Normanton – the Empire at Airedale, the Plaza at Fitzwilliam, the Alexandra and the Crescent at Pontefract, the Albion, Picture House and Queen's, Castleford, the Regent, Upton, and the Coliseum, Wakefield.

Of the major national circuits, Gaumont took over two cinemas in Wakefield in the 1920s. The Associated British Cinema Corporation (ABC) added the Albion in Castleford to its circuit for a time from June 1932 and built a new cinema in Wakefield in 1935. Essoldo acquired the Theatre, the Playhouse and the Grand Electric in Wakefield in the late 1940s and early 1950s. There were never any Odeon cinemas in the Wakefield District.

By 1957 the cinema industry was in financial trouble. There was increasing competition from home-based television. Other factors, including the riotous behaviour of teenagers which discouraged other patrons, hastened the decline. Many of the buildings were showing serious signs of age but it was not easy to find the money for the necessary repairs. The West Riding County Council was increasingly cautious in renewing licences. Star, in particular, was formally warned of the need for the renewal of electrical installations. The Council also demanded 'ceiling certificates' in the case of a number of picture houses.

Closures followed with cinemas being converted into bingo halls, used more briefly for other forms of entertainment, being transformed for wholly different purposes or, simply, being demolished. For some, in particular those without architectural charm, few images, if indeed any, remain so that the quest for material for this book has been something of a challenge.

But a positive note in conclusion: the oldest remaining theatre building in the District, the Theatre Royal and Opera House in Wakefield, which had a period as a bingo hall, is now thriving and an extension is anticipated in 2008-9.

Kate Taylor

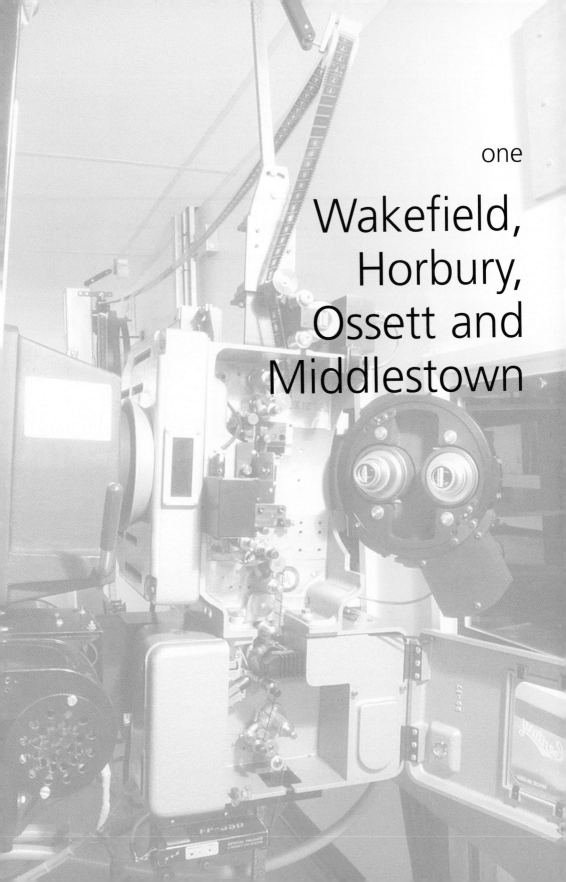

one

Wakefield, Horbury, Ossett and Middlestown

The first purpose-built theatre in the Wakefield District was opened in Westgate on 7 September 1776. It was built by James Banks, a wool-stapler whose fine Georgian town house still stands behind it facing Back Lane. The theatre was built for Tate Wilkinson (1739-1803) and was leased to him and, after his death, to his son John, to form part of Wilkinson's York Circuit. It was open for only a short period (from one to three weeks) in September each year at the time of Wakefield races which, in Wilkinson's day, were held on the Outwood. The first historian of the theatre, William Senior, provided a description of it as he knew it in the 1890s: 'The auditorium, like the outside, was plain and rectangular, and was capable of accommodating about a thousand people. The floor of the pit was level and the two tiers, very narrow at the sides and all but square at the corners, did not slope towards the stage after the manner of boxes and gallery in theatres of modern build, but were horizontal also. Bare rows of undivided benches were the boxes in the old days and, indeed, the utmost pinnacle of luxury the so-called dress circle at any time attained was represented by a few cane-bottomed chairs of the common pattern. The stage faced towards Westgate.' Wilkinson's company went on from Wakefield to Doncaster, for the race season there, and then to Hull for a thirteen-week winter stay. It then moved to its principal theatre, in York, before moving on to Leeds and then back to Wakefield. This drawing was done in the 1880s by Henry Clarke who was the surgeon at Wakefield Prison. The theatre was bought by Benjamin Sherwood in 1883 and named the Royal Opera House.

Tate Wilkinson (1739-1803) the actor manager who controlled the York theatre circuit for thirty-seven years. Until 1843 it was illegal to act for payment unless the company held a royal patent. Wilkinson had patents for both the Hull and York theatres, and, given that status, took only a modest risk in performing elsewhere. Whilst patent theatres were billed as Theatre Royal, elsewhere the simple title Theatre was used. After 1843 many theatres, without any real legitimacy, took the title Theatre Royal.

Tate Wilkinson, like other actor-managers of his day, engaged the stars of the London stage to perform with his company during the summer months when London theatres were closed. Sarah Siddons (1755-1831) was reputedly the greatest actress of the period. In 1886 Wilkinson was able to bring her to York, Hull and Leeds. There were complaints from his Wakefield patrons that they were not to see her there. Wilkinson consequently opened the theatre for one night, on 6 September. The prices of 5s, 3s and 2s were a substantial increase on the customary ones of 3s, 2s, and 1s and would equate with £100, £60 and £40 today.

M^{RS.} **SIDDONS,**

FOR ONE NIGHT ONLY.

THEATRE, WAKEFIELD.

On WEDNESDAY Evening, September 6, 1786,
Will be presented, a TRAGEDY, called

VENICE PRESERVED.

Jaffier,	Mr	CUMMINS
Duke,	Mr	WALLIS
Priuli,	Mr	LENG
Bedamar,	Mr	KNIGHT
Ranault,	Mr	MILLS
Spinofo,	Mr	BATES
Durand,	Mr	COLBY
Elliot,	Mr	NUNNS
Pierre,	Mr	KEMBLE

The Part of BELVIDERA, by

Mrs. SIDDONS.

To which will be added a FARCE, called,

MISS IN HER TEENS.

Fribble,	Mr	SOUTHGATE
Captain Lovet,	Mr	KAYNE
Puff,	Mr	COLBY
Captain Flash,	Mr	BATES
Tagg,	Mrs	LENG
Miss Biddy,	Mrs	MILLS

⁂ BOXES as at York (Mrs Siddons's Nights) 5s.—PIT 3s.—GAL. 2s.

Not any Places to be had without Tickets, which may be taken of Mr Swalwell, at the Theatre, from Twelve in the Morning till Two in the Afternoon.
To prevent Confusion, Servants are desired to be at the Theatre by Five o'Clock to keep Places.
The Doors will be opened at Six and begin at Seven o'Clock.
To prevent Delay, Ladies and Gentlemen are desired to bring Silver.—No Servants will be admitted without Paying; nor to keep Places after the first Act.
Not any Money returned after the Curtain is drawn up.

⁂ Mrs SIDDONS presents her most respectful Compliments to the Inhabitants of Wakefield, and its Environs, and assures them that Engagements made prior to those with Mr. Wilkinson, prevents her from staying more than this One Night; but she hopes when she has the good Fortune to revisit the County of York, that Time and Circumstances will allow her the Honor of extending her Performance in the Wakefield Theatre.

On SATURDAY,
The COUNTRY GIRL, with the ROMP.
By Mrs JORDAN, (for that Night only.)

MR. W. J. HAMMOND

Most respectfully begs to inform the GENTRY and INHABITANTS of WAKEFIELD and its VICINITY, that the
THEATRE WILL BE OPENED,

FOR A FORTNIGHT ONLY,

With a Superior Selection of Novelties.

THE PERFORMERS ENGAGED ARE—

Mr. STRICKLAND,	Mr. SLAITER,	Mr. MELVILLE,	Mr. OXBERRY.
Mr. JERROLD,	Mr. BARRETT,	Mr. CULLEN,	Mr. WILTON,
Mr. SHAW,	Mr. KELLY,	Mr. ANDREWS,	Mr. DEARLOVE.

Mr. C. BLAND—THE THREE BROTHERS RIDGWAY.

Miss PENLEY,	Miss MAYOSS,	Miss ANGELL,	Miss MEARS,
Miss LANCASTER,	Miss E. LANCASTER,	Miss ANDREWS,	Mrs. ANDREWS.
Mrs. MACNAMARA,	Mrs. W. J. HAMMOND,	Mrs. STRICKLAND.	

The Theatre has been partially re-painted and decorated by Mr. R. DONALDSON.
The Stage considerably improved by Mr. BRECKELL.

This present MONDAY, October 17th, 1831,
THE PERFORMANCES WILL COMMENCE WITH THE COMEDY OF

The Happiest Day of my Life.

Mr. Dudley, Mr. ANDREWS........Mr. Gillman, Mr. W. J. HAMMOND........Frederick, Mr. SHAW
Charles, Mr. J. RIDGWAY........Mr. Smith, Mr. JERROLD........Mr. Jones, Mr. WILTON
John, Mr. OXBERRY........Thomas, Mr. CULLEN
Mrs. Dudley, Mrs. MACNAMARA........Sophia, Miss PENLEY........Mary, Miss MAYOSS
Mrs. Grimley, Mrs. STRICKLAND........Mrs. Taylor, Miss SMITH........Jane, Miss LANCASTER
Miss Stokes, Miss ANDREWS........Miss Maddox, Mrs. ANDREWS

AFTER WHICH, A PETITE COMEDY, IN ONE ACT, CALLED

THE SECRET;

Or, The Hole in the Wall.

Mr. Dupuis........Mr. SHAW		Porter........Mr. CULLEN
Valere........Mr. J. RIDGWAY		Mrs. Dupuis........Miss PENLEY
Thomas........Mr. W. J. HAMMOND		Angelica........Miss MEARS

IN THE COURSE OF THE PIECE,
Mr. W. J. HAMMOND will sing, "WEDLOCK IS A TICKLISH THING."

To which will be added, a NEW BALLET DANCE, written and produced by the Messrs. RIDGWAY, called

ELECTRICITY;

OR, THE DOCTOR DOSED.

Lubin, in love with Lissette........Mr. J. RIDGWAY		Dame Horseleech........Mr. OXBERRY
Doctor Horseleech........Mr. T. RIDGWAY		Lissette........Miss E. LANCASTER
Pestle, his Man........Mr. G. RIDGWAY		Villagers, &c. &c.

IN THE COURSE OF THE BALLET,
A PAS DE DEUX, by Mr. J. RIDGWAY and Miss E. LANCASTER,

AND A COMIC EXTRAVAGANZA,

BY MESSRS. T. & G. RIDGWAY.

THE WHOLE TO CONCLUDE WITH THE

PROMISSORY NOTE;

Or, A Run before Breakfast.

Scamper........Mr. W. J. HAMMOND		Mrs. Markham........Miss MEARS
Mr. Markham........Mr. SHAW		Caroline........Miss MAYOSS
Nicks, a Bailiff........Mr. OXBERRY		Cicely........Miss LANCASTER
Bailiff's Follower........Mr. DEARLOVE		

On Tuesday, Auber's Grand Opera of MASANIELLO,
AND LUKE THE LABOURER.

AN ENGAGEMENT HAS BEEN CONCLUDED WITH THE CELEBRATED

MR. MATHEWS,

FOR POSITIVELY ONE NIGHT ONLY,
And he will have the Honor of making his FIRST APPEARANCE THESE FIVE YEARS, on SATURDAY next,
October 22nd, and publish his last Entertainment, called

THE COMIC ANNUAL.

PRICES——BOXES, 4s.—PIT, 2s.—GAL. 1s.——SECOND PRICE, BOXES, 2s.—PIT, 1s.
☞ Places to be had of Mr. HOPE, at the Box-Office.
✱✱✱ Doors to be opened at Half-past Six o'Clock, and the Performance to commence at Seven.

RICHARD NICHOLS, TYPOGRAPHER, WAKEFIELD.

Above: The varied and quite extensive evening's entertainment was typical of all theatres in the first half of the nineteenth century. William Hammond (1797-1850) was one of a number of actors whose tenure of the York Circuit was brief, in his case only for 1830-31.

Opposite above: In 1892 the West Riding County Council refused to renew the licence for the original Wakefield Theatre. It was demolished and the then owner, Benjamin Sherwood, built the present theatre on the same site. It was opened on 15 October 1894. The extension on the left, providing an unusually good scene dock, was completed in 1905.

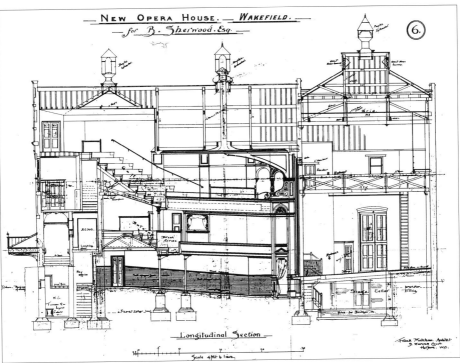

New Opera House. — Wakefield. —
— for B. Sherwood. Esq. —

Longitudinal Section

Scale 4 feet to 1 inch

Sherwood's choice of Frank Matcham (1854-1920) as the architect of his new theatre was an ambitious and far-sighted one. Matcham was among the most distinguished of all theatre architects. In 1889 he had designed the Grand Theatre in Halifax at no great distance from Wakefield.

Normally the fare at the Royal Opera House was provided on a weekly basis by professional touring companies bringing opera, musical comedy or drama. This amateur performance of *Not Such a Fool as He Looks*, written in 1869 by Henry James Byron (1834–1884), took place in 1904.

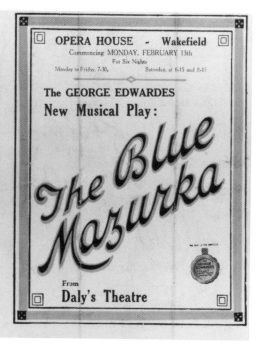

An advertisement of 1928. Daly's Theatre, in London, was from 1894 for almost thirty years the home of musicals. By this time the theatre was known simply as the Opera House.

ANDRASSY BROS., Wakefield.	**ROBERT WATSON** & SONS, Ltd., Wholesale Grocers, CHEAPSIDE, WAKEFIELD.	**The Steam Laundry** (WAKEFIELD) LTD., Quick Dry Cleaners.
Soft Drinks BY **E. P. SHAW'S.**	**THE SPENCER WIRE CO. LTD.,** Wire Manufacturers, THORNES, WAKEFIELD.	**T. MABANE &** **SONS, Ltd.,** 12, Bull Ring, WAKEFIELD.

EPISODE 3

Producer: MARGARET DAVIES.
PLAYED BY THE YOUTH DRAMATIC SOCIETY.

The Shepherds' Play from the Wakefield (Towneley) Mystery Plays.

ONLY four towns in England are known to have possessed a cycle of Mediaeval Town Plays—York, Chester, Coventry and Wakefield. Those of the other three are perhaps more famous, but Wakefield's contribution is full of Yorkshire wit and humour, and has many references to places in and around the town. The term "mystery" play means a play to be performed by a Trade ("mistere") or Craft Guild, and each Guild in the town undertook one play. These were usually stories from the Bible, interspersed with comedies such as the Shepherd's Play. They were performed on carts called "Pageants" which liverymen of the Guild dragged from point to point in the town, and the audience stood in the street to watch. Corpus Christi Day was the usual "Pageant Day."

Players in this Episode are:

Coll	Leslie Kendrew	Gill		Joyce Lee
Gib	Jack Lazenby	Herald		Wilfred Early
Daw	Dorothy Lee	Two property men	... Betty Bradshaw, Beryl White
Mak	Donald Sowden	Crowd	... Performers from Episode II

SOUND AMPLIFICATION **Lodge Radiovision,** LTD., 9, UPPER KIRKGATE.	**Westgate Motors** (WAKEFIELD) LTD., National Garage, WESTGATE, WAKEFIELD.	**J. E. FOWLER,** Electrical Contractor, 4, Bread Street, WAKEFIELD.
J. P. COCKER, Dental Surgeon, The Towers, Bond Street, WAKEFIELD.	**JOHN BROWN,** DRAPER, CROSS SQUARE.	**W. L. JACKSON,** Bedding Manufacturers, 9, Bank Street, WAKEFIELD.

PAGE SEVEN

Shortly before it changed hands in 1947, the Opera House hosted a pageant performed by a number of youth groups featuring the history of the city. This episode was drawn from the early fifteenth-century cycle of thirty-two 'mystery' (or craftsmen's) plays which were at one time performed in the streets of the town.

In the 1930s and 1940s provincial theatre had a difficult time competing with cinemas, especially after the coming of the 'Talkies' and the rise of stars. Like many other theatres, the Opera House survived on an increasingly cheap diet of resident repertory companies and low-brow revues. The Sherwood family sold the theatre to the Gateshead Empire Palace Ltd, in 1947. It was renamed the Essoldo and in 1954 was converted into a cinema, reopening on 24 January 1955 with the Cinemascope film *The Robe*. When the cinema closed on 5 February 1966 it passed to Essoldo (Bingo) Ltd. In 1973 the Ladbroke Group acquired it along with other Essoldo properties. It was then run as Lucky Seven bingo.

Opposite above: Apart from putting in a mezzanine floor above the stage, Ladbroke's preserved the theatre very well.

Opposite below: Moves to revive the theatre began in earnest in 1981 when local businessman Rodney Walker (later Sir Rodney Walker) called a public meeting to put forward a scheme to buy and reinstate the building.

Local government as well as many voluntary organisations backed the move. The photograph shows the restored theatre ready for its reopening on 16 March 1986 when a variety show was presented in honour

of the short-lived West Yorkshire County Council. With royal approval the theatre then became the
Theatre Royal and Opera House.

Tony Lidington (left), the theatre director, and Arthur Starkie, chair of the Centenary Committee, in front of a new backdrop on the stage of the Theatre Royal during the centenary celebrations in 1994.

In 1908 the Sherwoods commissioned Frank Matcham to design a Music Hall and Variety theatre for the narrow site to the right of the Opera House. Their new theatre was, however, built on a different site on the opposite side of the town. Planning permission was granted in 2006 for an extension to the theatre on this site.

Right: Little is known of what is referred to as the Corn Market theatre, occupying an upper floor of a warehouse in the York Hotel Yard. In 1850 it was opened briefly as Brears Concert Rooms.

Below: The theatre at the West Riding Pauper Lunatic Asylum was built by the West Riding magistrates in 1859 initially as a dining and recreation hall. By the 1860s balls were being held there. There were also irregular theatrical productions at which 600 could be seated. It was sometimes billed jocularly as the Theatre Royal, Stanley-cum-Wrenthorpe. W.S. Gilbert brought his play, *Acis and Galatea* there in the spring of 1875. The building was extended in 1893 with a new stage and, beneath it, dressing rooms. A projection box was added much later so that patients could enjoy films.

After the Theatre Royal became an Essoldo cinema, the hospital theatre was regarded as having the best stage in Wakefield. In the middle decades of the twentieth century hospital staff put on pantomimes there. The scene here is from the production of *Cinderella* in February 1964. A strike by ancillary staff led to the cancellation of the 1979 performances and the pantomimes came to an end. Later in the twentieth century, the theatre became a sports hall for hospital staff.

The Asylum, later named Stanley Royd Hospital, closed in 1995. The theatre was sold and was converted in 2006 for use by Destiny Church as a place of worship. This view is looking from the stage in June 2006.

Looking toward the stage of the Stanley Royd theatre during conversion, June 2006.

Destiny Church was opened on 18 November 2006 in the former Theatre at Stanley Royd Hospital.

THE

Empire ✦ Theatre,
BOROUGH MARKET, WAKEFIELD.

Open Nightly, with Crowded Houses and Enthusiastic Delight.

THE

BEST TALENT IN VARIETY ENTERTAINMENT
REGARDLESS OF EXPENSE.

S P E C I A L I T I E S   O F   A L L   K I N D S
AND

STAR ✦ ARTISTES
FROM ALL PARTS OF THE WORLD.

FRESH PROGRAMME WEEKLY.

Ballad, Operatic, Comedian, and Instrumental Music.
Burlesque Sketches. Pantomime Scenes.
Acrobatic Feats, Rare Exhibitions, New Ballet,
Skirt and Society Dances.

"MIRTH WITH REFINEMENT," Our Motto.

REFRESHMENTS (non-alcoholic) **on the Premises.**
CIGARS, &c.

Splendid Prize Band of Eleven Performers,
For Accompaniments and Selections.

Popular Prices for Admission:
1s., 9d., 6d, and 3d
Proprietor, WILL HEBDEN.

The first real rival in Wakefield to the Theatre Royal/Opera House was the Empire in Teall Street, close to Wakefield markets. It was a cheaply built, wooden pre-fabricated structure by T.V. Woodhouse of Nottingham. It measured some 90ft by 70ft and was said to be capable of holding 2,000 people in galleries, a pit, cushioned stalls and a promenade. It opened first as Baron Antonio's Grand Circus, on 28 September 1890 and advertised a programme of equestrian entertainment, acrobats and trapeze artistes, clowns and musical items with seats at 2s, 1s 6d, and 4d. After short tenancies by Edwin Croueste and James Comerford (known professionally as Zaro) the building was leased to Will Hebden in 1894 and run as a variety theatre under the name of the People's Empire. It was at first a great popular success. Hebden won favour too with Wakefield's middle class by putting on performances on behalf of good causes like the Free Library movement. In February 1895, the Mayor of Wakefield, Alderman Rhodes, claimed that the attractions of the Empire kept people out of public houses on Saturday nights and that 'there was now so little drunkenness in the town that the magistrates had scarcely anything to do on Monday mornings'. Quite who spread the rumour in 1896 that the Empire was unsafe can never be known. When he filed a petition for bankruptcy in February 1897, Hebden claimed that as the cause. Meanwhile Comerford had reoccupied the theatre and it was there, during a variety entertainment in December 1896, that moving pictures were shown for the first time in Wakefield. Determined to stifle the competition, Benjamin Sherwood, proprietor of the Opera House, managed to buy the building in 1897 simply to close it. It was let to the Wakefield Bill Posting Company and used as a vast advertising hoarding.

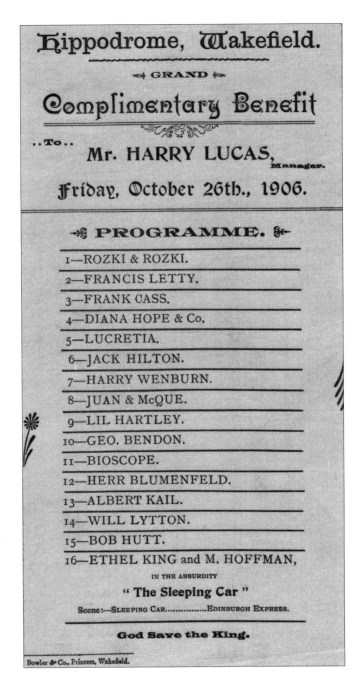

Hippodrome, Wakefield.

GRAND

Complimentary Benefit

..To..

Mr. HARRY LUCAS, Manager.

Friday, October 26th., 1906.

PROGRAMME.

1—ROZKI & ROZKI.

2—FRANCIS LETTY.

3—FRANK CASS.

4—DIANA HOPE & Co,

5—LUCRETIA.

6—JACK HILTON.

7—HARRY WENBURN.

8—JUAN & McQUE.

9—LIL HARTLEY.

10—GEO. BENDON.

11—BIOSCOPE.

12—HERR BLUMENFELD.

13—ALBERT KAIL.

14—WILL LYTTON.

15—BOB HUTT.

16—ETHEL KING and M. HOFFMAN,

IN THE ABSURDITY

" The Sleeping Car "

Scene:—SLEEPING CAR...............EDINBURGH EXPRESS.

God Save the King.

Bowler & Co., Printers, Wakefield.

In 1903 a second prefabricated building, very similar to the People's Empire, was erected close to it and opened on 28 December 1903 as the Hippodrome. The Sherwood family briefly reopened its neighbour. The owners of the Hippodrome went into liquidation in 1904 and the Sherwoods contemplated buying it, too, to close it down! However, it was acquired by a group of Wakefield businessmen (creditors of the bankrupt company) and, when Sydney Tolfree came to manage it as a Music Hall in November 1905, rivalry became keen and far reaching. Moving pictures, referred to as 'Bioscope', became a regular feature of the programme at the Hippodrome.

This page: Sydney Tolfree was the manager of the Hippodrome. In 1910, when the 1909 Cinema Act came into force, the Hippodrome was one of the first places in Wakefield to secure a licence. It was described at the time as having 320 tip-up seats and 23 rail-back seats. Increasingly stringent demands by the local authority led to its closure on 19 August 1922. It was sold at auction and ended its days as a rhubarb-forcing shed at a farm at Brandy Carr. The sale included two Kalee and three Gaumont chrono projectors and an almost new piano. On the bottom left is the only known image of the Hippodrome, taken from plans by T.V. Woodhouse.

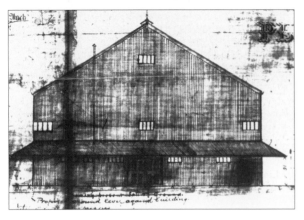

HIPPODROME

WAKEFIELD.

MANAGER	SYDNEY TOLFREE.
ASSISTANT MANAGER	HARRY HEATH.

THE PREMIER

PICTURE

PALACE.

One Standard only, THE Best.

**THE RECOGNISED FAMILY .
PLACE OF ENTERTAINMENT.**

ALWAYS UP-TO-DATE.

7   EMPIRE,   9

Kirkgate, Wakefield.

TWICE NIGHTLY.

SATURDAY EVENINGS 6-15 & 8-15.

ADMITTED BY PRESS AND PUBLIC TO BE THE MOST PERFECT
AND COMFORTABLE MUSIC HALL OUT OF LONDON.

THE UNIQUE SYSTEM OF VENTILATION MAKES THE EMPIRE
A BEAUTIFULLY COOL RETREAT IN THE SUMMER.

ENORMOUS CORONATION PROGRAMME.

NO INCREASE IN PRICES.

Occasions of national celebration, in particular coronations, were marked in theatres and cinemas by what purported to be special programmes. Here the coronation of George V is celebrated at the Kirkgate Empire. The theatre was built by the owners of Wakefield Theatre Royal and Opera House as a variety theatre in a deliberate attempt to put the Hippodrome out of business. Like the Sherwoods' 1894 Theatre, it was designed by Frank Matcham. The foundation stone was laid by Vesta Tilley on 8 October 1909 and the venue opened on 20 December of the same year. Moving pictures were a regular feature of the otherwise-live bill.

In May 1921, the Empire was acquired by the Leeds company, New Century. It was re-opened as the Empire Super Cinema on 25 July with *Kismet*. It was taken over by Gaumont in 1928 and renamed in 1950. *Up Front* was screened in 1951.

The Great Raymond Show appeared at the Empire in the week beginning 2 May 1910.

One Good Turn was shown in 1954. The cinema closed on 30 July 1960 and has since been demolished.

A branch of the Gaumont British Junior Club was founded at the Empire on 8 December 1945. The Club was 'opened' by the then Mayor of Wakefield, Cllr Mrs Effie Crowe.

Right: Joe Haigh in the projection room at the Empire. Joe worked in the cinema industry for thirty-four years. In his early years at the Empire, one of his tasks was to ferry the newsreels between it and the nearby Carlton.

Below: Robert Hall (right) with B. Megson, B. Dunford and W. Armitage in the Empire projection room.

Above: The Grand Electric. Wakefield's first permanent cinema was a conversion of the upper floor of the Corn Exchange. This had been built in 1837-8 at a time when Wakefield was a major centre for the corn trade. Corn was brought from eastern counties by barge up the Aire and Calder Navigation, sold via samples brought to the Exchange, and then carried across the trans-Pennine waterways to the industrial areas to the west. The cinema was opened on 22 December 1910. Known first just as the Electric, it gained the name Grand Electric in 1911. The upper-floor saloon, shown here as the cinema, had been in regular use throughout the Victorian period for political and social events and entertainment. Numerous bazaars had been held here for good causes such as the Wakefield Church Institution. John Bright spoke here on the evil of the Corn Laws in April 1843. Jenny Lind, the 'Swedish Nightingale', sang here in 1856. In 1958 Charles Dickens read *The Christmas Carol* here to 'a numerous, select and appreciative audience'. The D'Oyly Carte Opera Company gave *The Yeoman of the Guard* and the *Gondoliers* there in 1889 and 1890. Dioramas were exhibited there prior to its conversion into a permanent cinema; there had been earlier seasons of short films provided by itinerant exhibitors such as the New Era Animated Picture Company and the St Louis Animated Picture Company. As the Electric Cinema, it was fitted with fixed, tip-up seating but projection was at first simply from a fire-proofed stand in the auditorium itself. In 1929 the Corn Exchange was sold by auction. It was acquired by the Tolfree family, proprietors of the Playhouse, for use as their second cinema. Whilst leading feature films were shown at the Playhouse, the Westerns which came with them in the rented package were screened at the Grand Electric. Thus it acquired the nickname the Ranch-house.

Opposite above: The Corn Exchange/Grand Electric at the time of the visit to Wakefield of King George V and Queen Mary in July 1912.

The Corn Exchange in 1929.

Westgate, *c.* 1912. The Theatre Royal and Opera House is just to the right of centre. The store on the right, J.E. Hinchliffe, was acquired to be demolished and replaced by the Playhouse cinema.

Opposite above: The Playhouse was Wakefield's first purpose-built cinema. Its genesis lay in the continuing rivalry between Sydney Tolfree, who ran the Hippodrome, and the Sherwoods who owned both the 1894 Theatre Royal and Opera House and the 1909 Empire. Losing his variety audience to the upmarket Empire, Tolfree decided to invest in the developing cinema industry on a site close to the Theatre Royal. He formed the Wakefield Picture House Company and engaged Manchester architect Albert Winstanley to design the building. Known when it opened on 22 December 1913 as the Picture House, its name was changed to the Playhouse in 1915 when the Sherwoods, still engaged in hostilities, decided to put on films in their Theatre and Tolfree responded by bringing live repertory to the cinema.

Tolfree's Picture House was separated from the Sherwoods' Theatre by two shops. The theatrical terminology 'pit' was still being used in the 1920s.

Left: The programme for the Playhouse for the week beginning 15 March 1917 when Harry Russell's pantomime of Cinderella was being staged.

Below: As more cinemas were built in 1920 and 1921, the Tolfrees responded by renewing the interior of the Playhouse and introducing a cinema organ. The organ was first heard on 21 July 1921 when David Clegg, organist at the Winter Gardens, Blackpool gave a recital. The organ was a 3-manual Conacher with 2,000 pipes ranging from ones of a few inches in height to 16ft and with a 21-note tubular chime.

Monday, May 10th   **For 6 Days Only**

GRAND CORONATION PROGRAMME

GARY COOPER
WITH
MADELEINE CARROLL
IN

"THE GENERAL DIED AT DAWN" (A)

— ALSO —

MICKEY MOUSE, PARAMOUNT NEWS, ETC.

And **After** the Coronation—the Best Programme in Wakefield will Always be at THE PLAYHOUSE

Right: The coronation in question was that of George VI in 1937. The American film was released in 1936.

Below: A 'salvage matinee' at the Playhouse on 12 May 1945. Children under sixteen were admitted to a 10 a.m. performance upon an admission 'fee' of waste paper or books, the latter to be sent to members of HM Forces.

Both the Playhouse and the Grand Electric were taken over by Essoldo in 1956, thus giving Essoldo –
already owners of the Opera House – three cinemas in close proximity. *Mary Poppins* was released in 1964.

The Playhouse was acquired by Classic Cinemas when it bought out Essoldo in 1972. Subsequently the cinema had a chequered history. In November 1977 it was used as a skateboard centre, created by the removal of stalls seating, and from 8 p.m. as a 280-seat cinema.

The Playhouse closed finally in June 1978. It passed to Rank Leisure and became a nightclub. In 1997 it was acquired by the Barnsley-based firm Brook Leisure. It became famous throughout the nightclub world as Roof Top Gardens. It was completely refurbished in 2004 and renamed Quest. It won the UK nightclub of the year award in 2005. Mustang Sally's is an area within the nightclub which is based on a cowboy-town theme with a spit-and-sawdust feel.

Designed by Doncaster architect P.L. Treu for Ben Firth, the Carlton, in Grove Road, opened without ceremony on 14 September 1914. On the fringe of the city, it was Wakefield's second purpose-built cinema and held 1,100. Within three months, it was taken over by the Leeds-based company, New Century Pictures. On 21 December 1914 it became the first cinema in Wakefield to provide continuous entertainment from 6.30 p.m. to 10.30 p.m. rather than the customary two 'houses'. In the 1920s, New Century was taken over by Provincial Cinematograph Theatres (PCT) and this, in turn, was taken over by the Gaumont British Corporation in 1928. It closed on 29 September 1956 and was demolished.

Trinity Picture House, Belle Vue, was built for local entrepreneur Stephen Askew to the design of P.L. Treu and opened on 7 November 1914. Its original name reflected the proximity of Wakefield Trinity's Rugby League ground but it was variously advertised over the years as Belle Vue Palace, the Palace de Luxe and the Cosy Cinema, Belle Vue. It was nicknamed 'The Spit' or 'The Spit and Whistle' because of the notices displayed prominently on either side of the screen forbidding spitting and whistling – some indication of the habits of its patrons! Askew was not untypical of early cinema proprietors: a self-made man, he was ready to invest in any opportunity; he had an off-licence shop in Denmark Street and a boatyard at Wakefield Bridge running a business as a general canal carrier with his barge, Mary Jordan; he ran a passenger-boat service from York to the villages of Poppleton and Bishopthorpe; he had rowing boats on the River Ryton at Worksop. Throughout its years as a cinema, the Palace remained a family concern. During the 1914-1918 war, concerts were given in the cinema from time to time to raise funds for the families of men killed at the front (e.g. 19 May 1917). It closed on 6 September 1960. After a period as a bingo hall, it became a joinery workshop. In 2004 it was acquired as business premises by Printform.

Right: The Kine Year Book entry for Wakefield, 1922. The Tivoli was a conversion, in 1912, of the former Cocoa and Coffee Tavern in Stockdale Yard in Kirkgate. By 1921 it had difficulty satisfying the licensing authority and it closed, becoming for a time a stockroom for Marks and Spencer's. It is interesting to note that four of the cinemas listed here were managed by women.

Below: Stanley Picture House was the first of three cinemas opened in the Wakefield area shortly after the First World War. It was designed in 1919 by Woodlesford architect, E. Schofield, for a five-man partnership including Bottomboat clog manufacturer William Lamb and Stanley's market gardener John Edward Jacques of Hatfield Farm. It opened in 1920 and was swiftly nicknamed 'The Clog and Rhubarb'. It had 433 seats.

WAKEFIELD, Pop. 52,892.

CARLTON PICTURE HOUSE, Grove Road.—Prop. New Century Pictures, Ltd. Res. Man., T. Walshaw. Continuous. Two changes weekly. Phone, Wakefield 535. Station, Wakefield, L. & Y.R.

EMPIRE, Kirkgate.—Prop., Empire (Wakefield), Ltd. Res. Man., H. Norcliffe. Two shows nightly. One change weekly. Prices, 3d. to 1s. 6d. Phone, Wakefield 418. Station, Kirkgate, L. & Y.R.

GRAND ELECTRIC, Westgate.—Prop., Executors of late J. H. Hill. Res. Man., Miss F. E. Hardman. Two shows nightly. Three mats. weekly. Two changes weekly. Prices, 3d. to 1s. 3d. Station, Westgate, G.N.R.

HIPPODROME, Teall Street.—Prop., Pemberton and Penrice. Res. Man., F. King. Two shows nightly. Two changes weekly. Prices, 3d. to 9d. Phone, Wakefield 515. Station, Westgate, G.N.R.

OPERA HOUSE.—Prop., Sherwood & Co. Res. Man., Emily Sherwood. Phone, Wakefield 152. Station, Westgate, G.N.R.

PALACE, Belle Vue.—Prop., W. Askew. Res. Man., Mrs. Askew. Continuous. Two changes weekly. Prices, 3d. to 9d. Station, Kirkgate, L. & Y.R.

PLAYHOUSE, Westgate.—Prop., H. A. Close and S. Tolfree. Res. Man., C. Shayler. Two shows nightly. Two changes weekly. Prices, 5d. to 1s. 3d. Phone, Wakefield 240. Station, Wakefield, G.N.R.

TIVOLI PICTURE PALACE, Kirkgate.—Prop., Booth Grainge. Res. Man., Mrs. Bailey. Continuous. Two changes weekly. Prices, 4d. to 9d. Station, Westgate, G.N.R.

Above: In due course Jacques bought out his fellow directors. Jacques' daughter married projectionist Thomas Nettleton Howe who became his father-in-law's business successor. *Scarface* was released in 1932. The Picture House remained in Howe's hands until it closed on 31 December 1960.

Left: Stanley Picture House subsequently became a petrol station and remains in use as a motor-repair workshop.

The Coliseum at the Wakefield suburb of Eastmoor was established by local builder William Bagnall. Designed as a simple rectangular box by W.F. Peters of Woodlesford, it opened in November 1920. Seating was on wooden forms and the screen was painted on the rear wall. It changed hands and name more frequently

than any other cinema in the District. It was taken over by the growing chain Star Cinemas in 1933 and renamed The Star. A new screen was installed together with two Kalee projectors and BTH sound apparatus. It reopened on 4 December with Laurel and Hardy in *Fra Diavolo*. In 1945 it was sold to Parkrow Cinemas of Leeds and became the Rex. It closed on 7 February 1959. Ironically the last film shown was *The Killing*. *Her First Mate*, the film advertised here, was screened in 1934. It starred Slim Summerville and Zasu Pitts. The director was William Wyler.

The films *The Private Secretary* and *Dinky* were released in 1935.

Above: The Rex was bought by Leslie Teale in 1959 and was converted into a ballroom. Its modest rake was levelled and a sprung maple dance floor was installed.

Below: Teale leased the property to ballroom-dancing champion Harold Hulley who, with his partner Doreen Edwards, provided lessons. In the mid 1960s both Victor Sylvester and Margot Fonteyn came to the Rex for meetings of the International Society of Teachers of Dancing. A young man by the name of Paul Raven sang at the Rex; he was later to take the name Gary Glitter.

The attractions of ballroom dancing faded and in 1966 the lease of the Rex was sold to Bartle Enterprises, a local firm running bingo ventures at a number of other local venues.

In the late 1990s the Rex Cinema was sold to Everlux for use as a snooker hall.

Outwood Empire, built by the proprietors of 1913 Rothwell Empire only a few miles away, was opened in 1921. Its first manager, Reg Harrison, remained there until the cinema closed on 1 August 1964. It was sold to Bartle Enterprises, for bingo, in 1967.

Above: The Outwood Empire in 2006 as a drive through fish-and-chip restaurant.

Opposite above: In the 1920s and 1930s, Wakefield Corporation built, at Lupset, one of the largest housing estates in Europe. The Anglicans, the Roman Catholics, the Primitive Methodists and the Wesleyan Methodists all built places of worship there. Wesley Hall, at the junction of Thornes Road and Horbury Road, was unique in that the principal worship space had a raked floor, a raked gallery and a projection box, all remarkably similar to a picture house. Anonymously at the time, the cinema and film magnate J. Arthur Rank, who was himself a Wesleyan Methodist, gave £16,000 towards its cost.

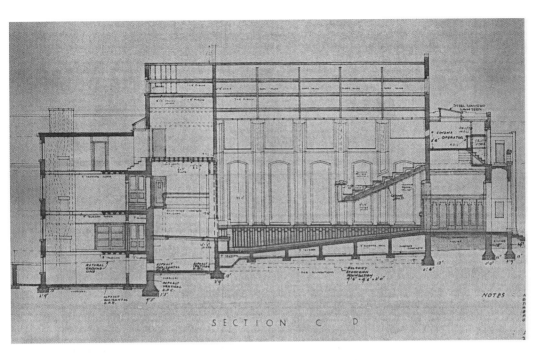

SECTION C D

The cinema-like worship space at Wesley Hall. By the 1990s the Chapel complex was far too large. It was demolished and the new West Wakefield Methodist Church was opened on a part of the site in 2003.

The Regal was opened by the Associated British Picture Corporation on 9 December 1935. Standing at the corner of Sun Lane and Kirkgate, it formed a centrepiece for the local authority's redevelopment scheme for this part of Wakefield. It was designed by W.R. Glen and had a seating capacity of 1,700. The authority itself opened quite palatial swimming baths nearby in 1938. *His Majesty O'Keefe*, starring Burt Lancaster, was released in 1954.

The foyer of the Regal in 1935.

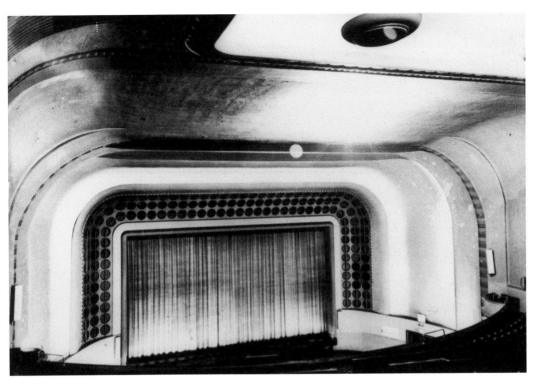

The auditorium of the Regal in 1935, looking towards the proscenium.

The Regal auditorium in 1935 looking towards the circle.

The Regal in 1937 celebrating the coronation of George VI.

An ABC Minors' Club event, *c.* 1960. The club was formed at the Regal on 17 July 1948 with a Saturday morning showing of *Gullivers Travels* and episode one of *Adventures of Rex and Rinty*.

Emile Ford in the manager's office at The Regal on 15 October 1960. Reg Helley, standing behind the young star, was manager from 1956 to 1961. Among Ford's greatest hits, with the Checkmates, was *On a Slow Boat to China*.

Members of the Regal cleaning staff at a training session in the circle foyer.

Donald Issatt, one of the projectionists at the Regal, in the projection room in the 1960s. The projector is a Ross with RCA sound and Peerless arc lamps.

Left: One of the live shows that were a feature of the Regal/ABC in the early 1960s. Manfred Mann's band was formed in 1962.

Opposite above: The West Riding Amateur Operatic Society took the Regal for a week annually from 1965 until the cinema was tripled in 1976. *Show Boat* was the first of these productions.

Opposite below: The West Riding production of *The Student Prince* on the stage of the Regal in 1974.

The Savoy was the last cinema to be built in Wakefield until the advent of the multiplex. The plot on which it was built was designated as a site for a cinema by Wakefield Corporation as a part of its vast, and prestigious, Lupset housing scheme. The Council recognised that there would be less resistance to slum clearance if they could provide the families who were being resettled with some of the amenities they had enjoyed in the centre of the town. (Plots were set aside too for four public houses and three fish-and-chip shops.) The site was taken by a Huddersfield company under the chairmanship of Mark Freedman, a man with twenty-four years' experience in the cinema business. Originally a tailor, his first venture as a picture-hall proprietor was in 1911 when he converted an old toffee works in Viaduct Street, Huddersfield. The Wakefield Picture House Company, anxious to quash any rival, opposed the Lupset cinema scheme. However it went ahead with a Huddersfield architect, Geoffrey Haigh, designing the rectangular building with a single storey, raked auditorium holding 1,020. The Savoy was formally opened by the Mayor of Wakefield, Alderman Albany Charlesworth, on 6 January 1936.

Opposite above: EMI took over the ABC circuit in January 1969. The cinema was tripled in 1976. The last films to be shown in the old 1700-seat auditorium, shown here just prior to tripling, were *Aces High* and *The Best of Benny Hill* on Saturday 30 October 1976. The tripled cinema reopened on 11 November. In December 1979, EMI was taken over by the electrical giant Thorn, forming a new company, Thorn EMI. In 1986 the Regal became the Cannon when that company, which had earlier acquired the Classic and Star chains, took over the Thorn EMI cinemas too.

Opposite below: The tripled Regal cinema in January 1997 displaying the new ABC logo which was used from 1996 when a new company was formed under a management buy-out.

- SAVOY CINEMA -

OPENING PROGRAMME

6th day of January, 1936, at 8 p.m.

·····························

1—NATIONAL ANTHEM.

2—**Official Opening Ceremony**

Kindly performed by His Worship the Mayor of Wakefield—
Alderman A. Charlesworth, J.P., assisted by the Mayoress.

3—INTERLUDE.

4—LAUREL & HARDY
in—
"GOING BYE-BYE" (a).

5—AFRICA—Land of Contrasts (u).
Travel.

6—UNIVERSAL NEWS.

7—OUR GANG
in—
"MAMMA'S LITTLE PIRATE" (u).

8—ON THE STAGE :
SYD PEARCE AND HIS BAND
with Colin Burke, Teddy Fawcett and MISS BOBBY LITTLE.

9—JOAN CRAWFORD and ROBERT MONTGOMERY
in—
"NO MORE LADIES" (a).

10—NATIONAL ANTHEM.

Left: A page from the souvenir booklet issued to patrons on the opening evening of the Savoy.

Below: The Savoy followed a similar pattern to many other cinemas in the late 1950s and the 1960s. It closed on 7 March 1959, but reopened on 5 February 1960 with the additional attraction of a Flamenco Coffee Bar. In 1961 entertainment was diversified with a bingo social club on Sunday and Monday evenings. The last films were screened on 24 February 1962. The BTH projectors were then transferred to the Hyde Park cinema in Leeds. The Savoy reopened in January 1963 as a bowling alley. Finally, in January 1973, it became a bingo club. It was destroyed by fire on 18 May 1993 and is pictured here during demolition.

Right: From its purchase by Wakefield Corporation in 1954 until it was sold again in 1984, the former Primitive Methodist Chapel, in Market Street, served as a theatre for amateur groups. The chapel originated in 1838 but was enlarged in 1880. The façade shown here dates from that time. The conversion to a theatre included creating a new entrance in Queen Street at the rear of what had been the chapel. Wakefield Little Theatre, which had been formed in 1947 (originally named the Chantry Players) put on productions here regularly.

Below: The interior of the Queen Street Hall.

Above: A scene from the Wakefield Little Theatre revue, *Nuts in May*, in May 1968. Performing are (left to right) Gail Rogers, Doreen Bentley, Joan Hackney and Judith Longmate.

Left: Unity House, built for the Wakefield Industrial Cooperative Society in 1901, was acquired by Wakefield Corporation in 1972. For many years its hall was used by Wakefield West Riding Amateur Operatic Society, a group which was founded in 1955, as their theatre.

Cineworld opened the first of its two multiplex cinemas in the Wakefield District at Westgate Retail Park in December 1996.

The foyer of Cineworld. The multiplex had twelve screens but in 2006 three were closed to make way for two restaurants, Frankie & Benny's and Nando's.

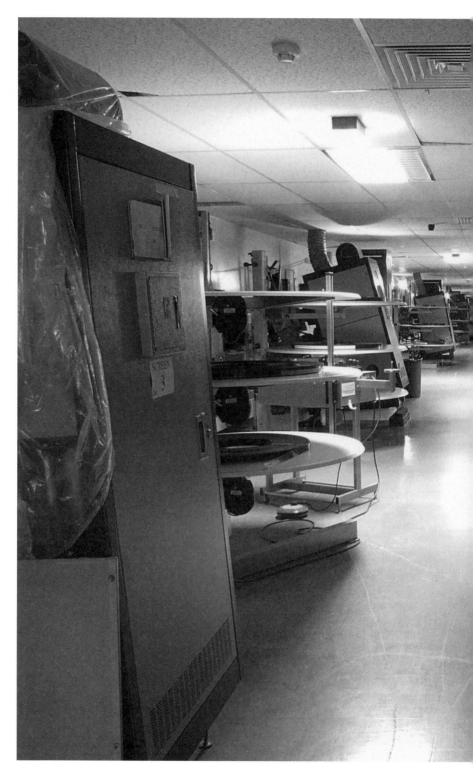

The vast projection room at Cineworld runs for the full length of the building.

One of the Strong platters which hold the reels of film is seen in the left foreground.

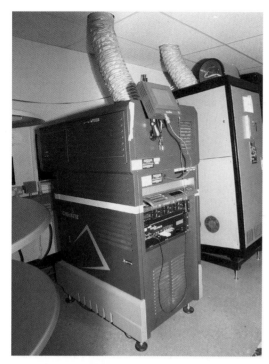

Left: The digital projector installed at Cineworld in 2006 at a time when the company was considering making a change more extensively to digital projection.

Below: One of the stadium auditoria.

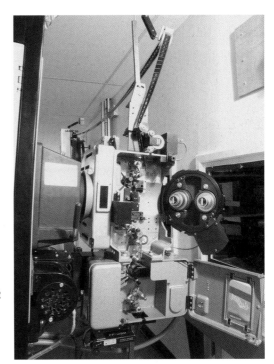

Right: Looking inside one of the projectors at Cineworld. The machine is a Strong Highlight 2 with a Century projector head.

Below: The operators' workbench in the Cineworld projection room.

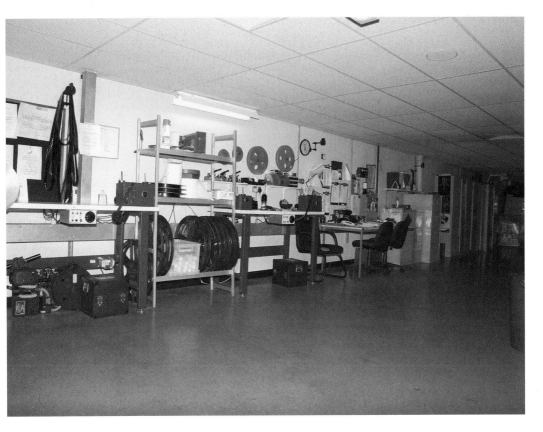

Horbury Co-operative Society was founded in 1866. In 1877 substantial premises were built at the junction of High Street and School Lane with an assembly hall on the first floor above the retail stores. From at least the 1890s the hall was used for theatrical performances and magic lantern shows and, by the turn of the century, for moving pictures. The Co-operative movement in general was strongly in favour of films as a means of education. The hall was licensed as a cinema from 1912. In 1915 it was let as the Horbury Electric Picture Hall with a seating capacity of 400. In 1927 the Co-operative Society took the cinema over again itself, deciding two years later to build a new cinema on land in School Lane. This was to be the first purpose-built cinema commissioned by a Co-operative Society. It was designed by the Horbury Urban District Council architect, William Sugars. The new cinema opened on 23 October 1930. Plans were submitted in 1922 by a rival concern for a picture house in Twitch Hill but the scheme came to nothing.

Horbury Cinema closed in July 1967. The manager said at the time that rowdy teenagers had discouraged any other audiences. It became a bingo hall and then stood empty for a long period before Peter Hunter opened it in 1992 as the Broadwalk Café, leisure centre for young people. It has since been demolished.

The mosaic floor of the foyer of Horbury cinema photographed in 1994 shortly before its demolition.

Above: Ossett Town Hall was licensed for the showing of films from 1910 and was run by the Newtown Picture Palace Company which already had a cinema in Cross Stamford Street, Leeds. It ceased to serve as a cinema when the Palladium was built.

Audiences at the Town Hall must have been encouraging as the Newtown Picture Palace Company, under its managing director Aaron Friedman, opened the purpose-built Ossett Palladium on 22 December 1913 with *Greater Love Hath No Man*. There was a formal opening on 6 January 1914. The Palladium was close to the Town Hall in Market Street. The *Ossett Observer* described it as 'a comfortable, pleasant building', and noted that it was well ventilated with an electric fan in the roof and that it was warmed by a 'hot water apparatus'. It could seat 800, principally on plush-covered tip-up seats. The first manager was John Wilson. Whilst he was on active service in the First World War, his wife took over the management. It remained an independent cinema until it closed on 29 April 1961. The managing director at the time was Aaron Friedman's son, Geoffrey. He said when it closed that the future for cinema lay with the large, luxury picture houses. The last film shown there was *The Miracle*. The building was demolished in March 1962. West Riding Picture Pavilions Ltd, a company formed by businessmen from Dewsbury and Heckmondwike, planned to build a cinema in Bank Street in 1913. Plans were drawn up by Heckmondwike architect Henry Stead but the scheme came to nothing.

Opposite below: The Temperance Hall, which had opened in Illingworth Street, Ossett, in 1888, may well have provided a venue for moving pictures on an ad hoc basis in the early 1900s. A cinema licence was issued on 28 December 1911 to J.T. Hawthorne. By 1920 the licence had been taken over by the Newtown Picture Palace Company, no doubt to end any competition. The West Riding County Council refused to renew the licence beyond 1922.

Opposite above: The reason for the crowds in Ossett Market Place is unknown. The Palladium is in the background.

Opposite below: Ossett Palladium in the 1920s.

Right: The interior of the Palladium.

Below: In 1970 a Compton-Christie theatre organ was installed in Ossett Town Hall. The major part of the organ was the Compton organ from the Rialto Cinema, Bebbington. However, organ parts from a number of other cinemas have been used too: The Cinema Organ Society notes that the piston relays and setter boards are from the Odeon, Swiss Cottage, and the Regal, St Leonards. The shutters are from the Greengates Cinema Bradford. The console is that of the New Victoria, London while the platform comes from the Plaza, Chorley. It was formally opened on 1 April 1970.

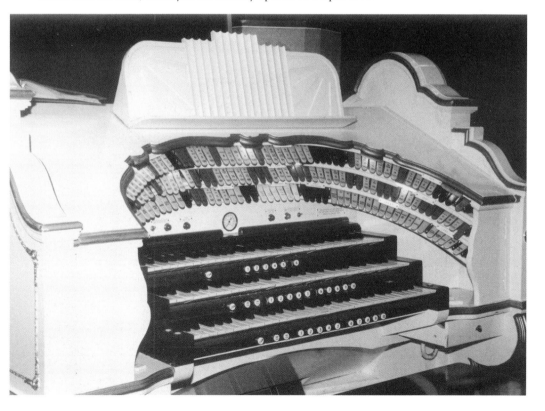

The Savoy Cinema in Middlestown was designed as an integral part of the new Co-operative Society building in 1930 and was run by the Society itself. The cinema entrance was in the centre of the front of the building with the greengrocery department on the left and the butcher's on the right. Losses in the 1950s and the investment that would be needed to install Cinemascope led to the cinema being offered for sale, fruitlessly, as a going concern in August 1958. It closed on 28 February 1959. Horrell Metcalfe, the Society's president, laid the blame for the decline in patronage to television.

The former Co-operative Society in the 1980s.

two

Castleford, Normanton, Glasshoughton and Airedale

The Theatre Royal, Castleford, was built about 1880 as a Salvation Army barracks. It was converted as Castleford's first permanent theatre in 1892. In 1911 the then owner, Charles Gadsby, undertook major alterations, employing the leading theatre architect Frank Matcham. These included adding a gallery and a canopy over the entrance as well as facing the front with Portland cement. At the same time Gadsby took his sons, Albert and Frederick, into partnership. A sale brochure of 1919 described the theatre as having an imposing main entrance with tiled floor, ticket office, and main staircase, with a separate entrance for the pit. It had seating for 980 in the pit, orchestra stalls, dress circle and gallery. There were bars on each floor. It had a good loading bay with the entrance from Wilson Street. It remained a live theatre until its closure in January 1955. Claude Hunter and Bernard Robshaw, both formerly clerks at Wheldale Colliery, reopened it on 24 December 1957 but their venture failed within three months. This photograph dates from that time. For a short period in 1958 it became a venue for boxing and wrestling matches. In 1959 it became Las Vegas Theatre and Restaurant. It was demolished in 1964.

tified Insane" and "The Skin Game"

The Company include :—

☆ MISS PHYLLIS CLAUDE.
☆ MISS CISSIE ASHLEY.
☆ MISS MAUDE LESLIE-CUDD.
☆ MISS MARGARET IVES.
☆ MISS ELIZABETH WEBB.

☆ Mr. LEONARD HARRISON.
☆ Mr. ARTHUR BARCLAY.
☆ Mr. EDWARD W. CUDD.
☆ Mr. LAWRENCE SCOTT.
☆ Mr. LAURENCE GRANT.
☆ Mr. RICHARD WEBB.
☆ Mr. JACK WEST.
☆ Mr. H. BROTHERTON RIVERS.
☆ Mr. CHARLES ATKINSON.

Business Manager : Ed. W. CUDD.

The Plays Produced and Directed by LEONARD HARRISON.

THEATRE ROYAL, CASTLEFORD.

FOR ONE WEEK ONLY. MONDAY, JANUARY 16th, 1928.
Once Nightly, Monday to Friday, at 7-30.   Saturday, Twice Nightly, at 6-30 & 8

LEONARD HARRISON PRESENTS
PLAYS AND PLAYERS.

MONDAY, TUESDAY, AND SATURDAY.
(at 7-30)   (6-30 & 8-45)
Castleford's Favourite Play :

"CERTIFIED INSANE
By EDITH CARTER.
Originally produced at the Royalty Theatre, Castleford
With Enormous Success !

WEDNESDAY, THURSDAY & FRIDAY.
Each Evening at 7-30.
JOHN GALSWORTHY'S DRAMATIC MASTERPIECE
(From the St. Martin's Theatre, London)

"THE SKIN GAME"
The greatest game on earth—doing your neighbour."
I guarantee Perfect Production and a First Class Company.
(Signed) LEONARD HARRISO

MR. LEONARD HARRISON

Above: For much of its life, a different touring company appeared at the Theatre Royal each week.

Right: In the 1930s and 1940s provincial theatres found it increasingly difficult to compete with picture houses since the latter, rather than touring companies, had the stars. They became increasingly dependent on seasons by repertory companies and on revues.

Moving pictures found their first permanent home in Castleford in the building which was variously known as the Queen's Hall, the Hippodrome, the Queen's Theatre of Varieties, and the Queen's Cinema. It was built by the Castleford Concert and Varieties Lecture Hall Company and was opened in 1899 as a variety theatre. It reopened as the Hippodrome on 31 October 1904 with short films as part of the programme. The next two years saw chequered fortunes but it began to prosper from 1906 when it was taken over by partners Charles H. Beanland and Will Emerson. The Queen's Theatre Company was formed to acquire it in 1909. The postcard dates from 1907.

From 1907 films were a regular part of Beanland and Emerson's variety bill. The Queen's remained a live theatre until 1931. It was then run as a cinema and was taken into the Star circuit in 1942. It closed on 25 January 1959. The last feature was *The Lone Ranger*. The building was taken over by Asda and served for a time as a supermarket before being demolished in 1990.

Above: In March 1939 a van advertising the Hughie Green show at Butlins toured the streets of Castleford but how far did the shadow of war deter bookings?

Below: In the early years of the cinema industry many public houses exhibited films. Castleford's Crimea Tavern was among them. It was granted a cinema licence by the West Riding County Council in both 1910 and 1911 but was refused a licence in 1912 when the council seems to have adopted a policy of banning moving pictures from all the public houses within the county.

The Empress Cinema was the first of four cinemas to open in Castleford in 1912. Coal mining communities – even quite small villages – across the country acquired picture houses at much the same time. It had begun life as the Empress Ballroom, built in 1907 on a site in Church Street which had been acquired by Dawson Waite, a cabinet maker, but which was converted for films and opened on 18 March 1912 under the management of Charles J. Cox, a Castleford electrical engineering contractor. In spite of, or perhaps even because of, the first national miners' strike, there were crowded 'houses'. It seated 700. Its screen was 16ft by 14ft. Seating prices depended in part on the floor covering: for 6d you got a carpet but linoleum was only 4d. The Empress closed suddenly in November 1921. The remaining episode of the serial *The Phantom Fox* was shown instead at the Star.

The Star Picture Palace in Aire Street was a conversion of existing premises beside the River Aire – probably a warehouse – and seated 700. It opened in 15 August 1912, advertising that it had the 'largest, best, brightest, steadiest and clearest' picture programme in the district. It was closed in July 1923 for refurbishment and for the construction of a gallery, and re-opened on 4 February 1924 as The Majestic. After closing in the summer of 1930 it reopened in October as the Astoria with Arthur Hellawell as its manager. After another closure in the summer of 1931, it was acquired by Walter Eckart, the first cinema of what was to become Eckart's extensive Star circuit and renamed the New Star. At one time, Star was the fourth largest circuit in Britain. In 1968 some £30,000 was spent in modernising the cinema. It closed suddenly on 8 June 1975 when *The Towering* Inferno was playing to capacity houses. The film was transferred to the Star-leased Albion which reopened as a triple cinema on 9 June 1975. The film advertised here, *The Way We Were,* was issued in 1973.

Above: The end of the European part of the Second World War, VE Day, provided this occasion for the Star to display a wealth of flags. The film that week, *Together Again*, starred Charles Boyer and Irene Dunne.

Left: All that remained of the Star at the Millennium in 2000 was this advertising board in Normanton.

The Albion, standing on the corner of Albion Street and Wilson Street, opened on 2 December 1912. The opening performance was billed as 'in aid of the Castleford Ambulance and Nursing Division'. It was a comparatively small cinema, the stalls and circle together having only 600 seats. It was built by a local builder, Joseph Craven, who had come to Castleford in the early 1870s to take advantage of the building opportunities resulting from the expansion of the mining industry. The active partner in the enterprise from the start was his second son Herbert. The two traded as the Castleford Electric Theatre Company. Castleford's fourth cinema of 1912 was the Crown, which opened at Christmas. This, too, was erected and at first run by a local builder, George H. Wilson, but was shortly sold to Arthur James Campy. Charles Cox took over the Crown in 1913. The managers of the Queen's Theatre, the Albion, the Empress and the Star had an agreement over the hiring of films so that they showed complementary programmes rather than adopting a cut-throat approach. Cox chose to act independently so the consortium attempted to put the Crown out of business. Their secretary, H. Coulthard, wrote to the film renters threatening to boycott them if they allowed Cox to have any new films. Lengthy advertisements for the Crown appeared in the new local paper, the *Elmsall and Hemsworth Express*, on 28 November and 5 December 1913 quoting from the trade paper, *The Cinema*, and giving details of the correspondence. As a result the consortium withdrew their advertising from the paper for some time. Outclassed by Castleford's 1921 Picture House, the Crown advertised in 1923, 'We are still keeping up our reputation for the finest pictures in Castleford,' and, 'The little Crown keeps pace with Yorkshire's finest cinema, the Majestic in Leeds'. But in the small hours of Saturday 5 May it suffered a devastating fire. Its floor was wooden and a fault in the alarm system meant that the Castleford fire brigade never turned out.

Picture Halls.

Archibald Ramsden's have a number of **Upright and Horizontal Grand Pianos** specially suited for the use of **Entertainers** and **Picture Houses.** The hard wear given to pianos in such places necessitates a specially reliable and lasting instrument, and whether you want an Upright Piano or a Grand, **Archibald Ramsden's have just the most suitable** piano for the purpose, with full, round, powerful, tone. Special prices are quoted by Archibald Ramsden's for this class of instrument.

FIFTY YEARS' REPUTATION FOR RELIABLE GOODS.

Archibald Ramsden, Ltd., 12, Park Row, Leeds.
Local Agent: J. HUDSON, 25, Carlton Street, Castleford.

Above: A newspaper advertisement in the *Pontefract and Castleford Express* in 1912. In the days before sound, many cinemas had a pianist to accompany the films. One pianist recalled getting a list each Monday morning of the music required, hurrying to buy the various items from a local music shop and returning to the cinema to practise before the doors opened to the public.

Below: Outclassed by the Picture House, the original Albion Cinema closed in 1927 when on 31 January 1927 its successor, built by the Craven family just a few doors away in Albion Street, opened. The first film in the new Albion was *The Son of the Sheik* with Rudolph Valentino. From 1932 it was leased to Associated British Cinemas. It was taken over by the ubiquitous Star in November 1957 and was tripled in 1975. Its final years as a cinema were under Cannon. It closed in 1987 and became a nightclub.

Above: The original Albion on the left with its successor on the extreme right, in 2006.

Right: In the 1930s and 1940s the circuit chains each had their own children's club. There were the ABC Minors, the Gaumont British Junior Club, the Odeon National Children's Club, the Granadiers Club, the Granada Rangers, and the Star Young Citizens Club.

Castleford's first four picture houses had little glamour. They were simply sizeable boxes with a screen and projection equipment. However by 1921, after the austerity of the First World War, audiences were looking for greater luxury. Castleford got its super cinema when the Picture House in Station Road opened on 29 August showing Mary Pickford in *Pollyanna*. It was designed by a leading Castleford figure, County Alderman Arthur Hartley JP and was built on a part of Beancroft. It made a splendid visual impact with its white faience exterior and mosaic dancing figures. The men behind the enterprise were rag merchants John Arthur Rowley of the Victoria Works, Batley, and Walter Townend of Ossett. They had first ventured into Castleford when, as the Victoria Picture Company, they ran both the Empress and the Star as tenants. In 1920 they formed a new company with Elliott Aspinall, using the initials of their three surnames, RTA. The company continued to operate the cinema until September 1962 when it was sold to Star and immediately closed down. The last film was *Follow that Dream* starring Elvis Presley. Star had tried and failed to purchase the Queen's Theatre, which was then running as a bingo hall. They opened the former Picture House as the Casino Bingo Club on 4 October 1962.

Above: The dancing figures on Castleford
Picture House.

Right: A detail from Castleford Picture
House.

CASTLEFORD AMUSEMENTS

NEW STAR
CASTLEFORD Tel. 2231

Week commencing
Monday, July 7th, 1947.
Nightly at 5.30 and 8.15.
Matinees Daily (except Fri.) at 2.30
Special Children's Matinee
Saturday at 2.15.

SIX Outstanding SIX
DAYS Attraction! DAYS

Tyrone Power
Gene Tierney
John Payne
Anne Baxter
Clifton Webb
Herbert Marshall
in

**THE
RAZOR'S EDGE**

Between love and hatred there
is a line as sharp as a razor's
edge! Superb drama based on
Somerset Maugham's best
selling novel.

Patrons please note early
times of starting.

Book early to avoid
disappointment.

QUEEN'S
CASTLEFORD Tel. 2268

Monday, July 7th, 1947,
Three Performance Daily,
2.15 — 5.30 — 7.45.
(No Matinee Friday)

Monday, Tuesday, Wednesday.

Roy Rogers
in

**SONG OF
ARIZONA**

The King of Cowboys in a
thrilling musical Western.

THE ARTEMUS BOYS in
**THE GRAND
ESCAPADE**

An exhilarating tale of three
boys in search of adventure.

Thursday, Friday, Saturday

Jack Lambert
in

**NINE
MEN**

Gripping adventure story of
self sacrifice and heroism.

JULIA LANG in
**CHILDREN ON
TRIAL**

A startling drama of juvenile
delinquency.

Don't forget Sunday opening
on July 6th.

PICTURE HOUSE
CASTLEFORD Tel. 2351

Week commencing
Monday, July 7th, 1947.
ALL THE WEEK
Daily at 2.30, 5.40, 8.0.
No Matinee Friday.

OUTSTANDING
PRODUCTION

Ernest Hemingway's Famous
Story

**THE
KILLERS**

Featuring

Edmond O'Brien
Ava Gardner
Albert Dekker
John Miljan

Raw, rugged drama in this
unusual murder mystery!

THEATRE ROYAL CASTLEFORD
—TELEPHONE 2715—

Week commencing Monday, July 7th, 1947.
6.15 p.m. and 8.15 p.m.

BAND BOX

A Cocktail of Music and Comedy, with
DOUGLAS COOPER AND HIS MUSIC
Introducing Peter Mills and Julia Hale.
KEITH WILBUR   TED LUNE   BOSTON TWO
B.B.C. Impressionist. Almost a Soldier, Youth in dancing mood
AND FULL SUPPORTING CAST.

Next week's show at the Theatre Royal Castleford is 'Band Box'
and the starring act is the well-known band Douglas Cooper and His
Music. They offer a cocktail of music and comedy, with Peter Mills and
Julia Hale as vocalists. Other acts in the show include the B.B.C.
impressionist Keith Wilbur; a 'magical act' by Condor and J.C.
Mavias; Mais and Mira with their 'fiddling and fooling' and Ted
Lune, who calls himself 'almost a soldier'. Ted Osborne getting
sentimental, and the Boston Two, showing youth in dancing mood
complete an attractive cast.

ALBION CASTLEFORD (Phone) 20521

Commencing July 7th, for 3 days.

WILL HAY in
OH MR. PORTER
Screened at 2.0, 5.30, 8.0.   (U)

Commencing July 10th, for 3 days.

JAMES CRAIG, LUCILLE BREMER in
CYNTHIA'S SECRET
Screened at 2.0, 5.30, 8.0.   (A)

NO MATINEE FRIDAY.   BOOK YOUR SEATS.

Will Hay, the schoolmaster comedian, with Moore Marriott and
Graham Moffatt, have a riotous time in Oh, Mr. Porter, one of the
main films at the Albion Cinema, Castleford, next week. Shunted to
small station in Northern Ireland, on which the local Irish believe the

---

Above: Advertisements for Castleford entertainments in the *Pontefract and Castleford Express* in 1947.

Left: Normanton Assembly Rooms were built in 1888. In 1910, when the act requiring the licensing of any venue showing moving pictures to a paying public came into force, its proprietors secured a licence. By July 1912 it was known as Normanton Picture Palace and was run by Messrs Dobito and Buxton (perhaps the same Buxton who built the Hippodrome in Featherstone) who provided a mixture of films and variety turns.

Opposite above: In 1920 the Assembly Rooms were sold to Normanton Theatres Ltd. This company left the Assembly Rooms for its purpose-built Majestic Cinema in 1931 when the opening film was *The Queen's Husband.* The Majestic was taken over by Star Cinemas in 1936 and closed on 20 June 1959.

In the 1960s the Majestic provided storage space for local authority vehicles.

Above: The purpose-built Grand Palace, later known just as the Grand, opened on Castleford Road, Normanton, in December 1912. The first films included *The Obligation*, which was said to have a special interest for miners. In the 1950s it was, like many other Wakefield District picture houses by this time, taken over by Star Cinemas. It closed in November 1957.

COSY Movie News
AND PROGRAMME

COSY CINEMA 'Phone 2350 Castleford
GLASSHOUGHTON,
CAR PARK.   MANAGER : L. ADDY.

Above: The Cosy Cinema, Glasshoughton, was the last picture house to open in the Wakefield District (in 1939) until the advent of the Cineworld multiplexes at the turn of the century. The builders were Turner Bros of Hemsworth. It closed initially in the summer of 1958 but, after protest from pensioners, reopened in September. It closed finally on 23 May 1959. Its owner at the time of closure was Ernest Freedman of Leeds.

Opposite below: Normanton Empire opened on 8 May 1913 and was a conversion of Harry Forbes's grocery shop. It seated 450. Like the Palace it initially offered a mixture of films and variety. It became part of the Star Circuit in the 1950s. It closed on 13 September 1964 and was for some years derelict. It was purchased in 1995 by Brian Ellis and converted into flats. It still retains its original 1890s shop front.

Above: Originally named the Grand, the Airedale Empire opened in 1929 with W.H. Jackson as the licensee. It became part of the Star chain in the 1950s. It had closed by 1960. It is pictured here in 2006.

Left: The Wayward Bus and the *Curse of Frankenstein* were released in 1957.

Opposite above: The entrance to the vast Xscape complex at Glasshoughton, near Castleford. Opened in October 2003, it rapidly became one of the most popular tourist attractions in the country.

The entrance to the fourteen-screen Cineworld is via an escalator from the ground floor of Xscape. Cineworld was founded in 1996. The company was acquired in 2004 by the Blackstone group which took over the UCG cinema chain at the same time.

The first-floor café/bar at Cineworld.

One of the four VIP boxes at Cineworld.

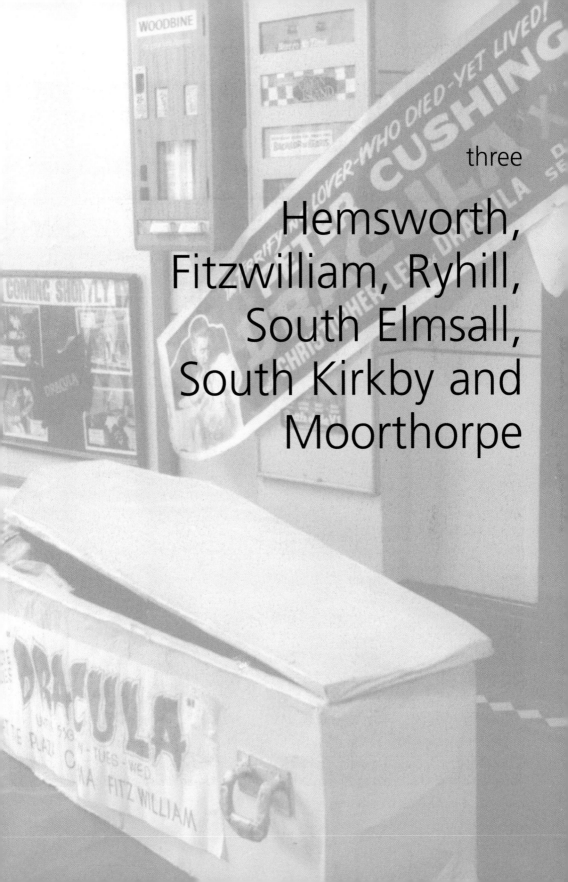

three

Hemsworth,
Fitzwilliam, Ryhill,
South Elmsall,
South Kirkby and
Moorthorpe

Hemsworth Hippodrome was built in Hague Lane (also known as Kirkby Road) in 1911 for the Hemsworth Hippodrome Company. The company directors included Sidney Gill and Cornelius Nelson. The company secretary was John Thomas Issott, proprietor of Moorthorpe Empire. The cinema had a café. It closed as a cinema in the 1960s.

The Hippodrome as a Bingo hall in 2006.

The Hippodrome auditorium furnished for bingo.

The Hippodrome stage providing further accommodation for bingo in 2006.

Above left: The Picture House, in Westfield Road, Hemsworth opened in 1922. The photograph was taken in 2006 when it provided a workshop for Woodall's motor engineering firm.

Above right: In 1924 the South Kirkby Cinemas Ltd bought a plot of land in Fitzwilliam from the Hemsworth Hall estate, building the Plaza cinema between the railway line and the road from Nostell to Kinsley. Its seating was divided between the stalls and 'balcony', the latter being simply a raised section at the rear of stalls. In 1930 its manager, Harry Austerfield, appeared before Pontefract magistrates for placing fifty-three chairs in the gallery aisle on Bank Holiday Monday, supposedly creating a hazard. Austerfield claimed that many other cinemas adopted the same practice. He admitted that there were empty seats in the front row of the stalls but said that nobody would sit in them. The cinema was taken over by Star in 1936. It closed on 29 October 1960 and has since been demolished.

VICTOR MATURE MICHAEL WILDING ANITA EKBERG

CinemaScope
and Technicolor

THE MIGHTY ZARAK

Mr Hurst (the second man from the right on the back row) organized an annual trip to Blackpool for the prizewinners in children's talent contests. This one took place in 1957.

Opposite below: The manager at Fitzwilliam Plaza from 1956 until its closure was Dennis Hurst, known to the Fitzwilliam Young People's Matinee Club as Uncle Peter. He made numerous models, like the dog here, to promote the films. The models were fashioned from chicken wire taken from the boxes of shot from a local colliery. They were then coated with hundreds of strips of newspaper soaked in paste (papier mâché) and then coated in a weatherproof oil paint.

Opposite above: Another group outside the Plaza gathered for a Blackpool trip. The young woman on the right, with her hands on the shoulders of the little girl in front, is Jean Dodd. Jean started work at the Plaza as the 're-wind boy' on a wage of £1 12s 6d a week and remained there as a projectionist (for the last three years as the only projectionist) until it closed.

Opposite below: Children outside the Plaza taking part in a competition for the best Buffalo Bill.

Right: A foyer promotion at the Plaza.

Below: A queue for a children's matinee at the Plaza.

As far as is known, the first season of films in Ryhill was at the National School and was promoted by Ellis Barraclough and R. Ingham. In 1913 Barraclough's father, George, built the Imperial Picturedrome on a vacant site bounded by Charles Street, Lafflands Lane and Back Lane. The site had earlier been used by a portable theatre which toured West Riding villages, William Kelso's Empire Music Hall. The Picturedrome measured 50ft by 30ft and was 20ft high. The auditorium had a barrel roof and a simple raked floor. There was a 12ft wide plaster screen. A lean-to at the side held a gas engine providing electricity for the arc lamps. The Picturedrome was unprofitable. It could never compete with Ryhill Empire. There is a story that Ernest Silverwood, proprietor of the Empire, posted his cinema bills on his Model T Ford. Ellis Barraclough posted bills on a handcard advertising that he could not afford a car. The Empire is reported to have closed on 31 July 1923. The cinema was converted into a piggery and slaughterhouse by Oswald Hepworth.

THE LAFLEUR THEATRE ORGAN

The most amazing musical invention of the age is undoubtedly the Lafleur Theatre Organ. Here is an organ without pipes, reeds or wind, all its sounds being produced entirely by electricity ... An ingenious system gives the organist nearly 250 million tones to choose from, all being obtainable from 9 controls. The familiar organ tones are available, and in addition many new ones. The range also includes Imitations of such instruments as the accordion, banjo, xylophone, tom-tom, etc. The Lafleur Theatre Organ will reproduce the music of the Cathedral Organ, the Symphony Orchestra and the Dance-Band, and is the most versatile musical instrument in existence. It is also one of the few that cannot go out of tune. The volume of tone can be varied to suit any building from a private residence to the largest super cinema.

The LAFLEUR THEATRE ORGAN has to be seen and heard to be believed, and cinema-goers are advised not to miss this opportunity given to them by the foresight of the EMPIRE RYHILL management, to hear this modern wonder.

STANLEY MILLER, who is playing the Lafleur Theatre Organ at the Empire Cinema, Ryhill, this week, has been a cinema organist since the days of silent films. He has held resident posts at Norwich, Cambridge and Dewsbury, and at Lambeth—home of the Walk.

Mr. Miller was the first cinema organist in Europe to play the new pipeless organ and he has become England's foremost exponent of this remarkable instrument. During the last two years he has given performances in a variety of places of entertainment, and was privileged to play at a Command Performance for H.M. Queen Mary at the Capitol, Cardiff. He has also given performances in the immense Stadium at Earl's Court and at the London Coliseum. He was very popular at Dewsbury, and looks forward to an enjoyable week in Ryhill.

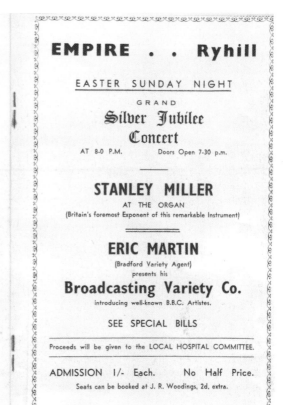

EMPIRE . . Ryhill

EASTER SUNDAY NIGHT

GRAND

Silver Jubilee Concert

AT 8-0 P.M.   Doors Open 7-30 p.m.

STANLEY MILLER

AT THE ORGAN

(Britain's foremost Exponent of this remarkable Instrument)

ERIC MARTIN

(Bradford Variety Agent)

presents his

Broadcasting Variety Co.

introducing well-known B.B.C. Artistes.

SEE SPECIAL BILLS

Proceeds will be given to the LOCAL HOSPITAL COMMITTEE.

ADMISSION 1/- Each.   No Half Price.

Seats can be booked at J. R. Woodings, 2d. extra.

Ryhill Empire was founded by Ernest Silverwood. It was opened on Easter Monday 1914. It is claimed that it was the first cinema in the region to install a British (rather than French or German) projector. A second, reconditioned and this time French, projector was installed only a little later so that the longer films of the time could be shown without a break whilst the reels were being changed. In the late 1920s Silverwood invested in a sound-on-disc system. This was unsatisfactory as were the two sound-on-film projectors he bought shortly afterwards. In 1933 the cinema was fitted with Western Electric wide-range sound. The cinema's silver jubilee was celebrated in some style at Easter 1939. The Empire was always a family business and in its last years was run by June Silverwood. It closed on 30 August 1959. It became a cold store for J.W. Swithenbank's frozen foods division. Silverwood also ran Silver Ace Motor Coaches, the Holm Valley garage and the Ryhill Cash Stores. The page shown here is from the cinema's Silver Jubilee souvenir brochure.

2. The New Empire, Moorthorpe.

Left: The Empire, Moorthorpe was built in 1912 for the Empire (Moorthorpe) Ltd and its managing director, John Thomas Issott. It was designed for both films and variety with a stage which was 57ft wide and 20ft deep. It held seating for 850 in the pit/stalls and 210 in the circle. It closed in 1919 and was reopened as the New Empire. Productions by the local amateur dramatic society were held here.

Below: The Empire closed as a cinema on 15 October 1968. It was then run as a bingo hall by Palace Enterprises of Castleford.

The vast fly-tower at Moorthorpe Empire.

In 2006 the Empire was converted as flats. The fly-tower forms part of the new complex

Staff outside the Picture Hall, or Picture House, South Elmsall, opened on or about 11 March 1911. It was built for the South Elmsall Picture Hall Company. The architect, Percy Archibald Hinchliffe, was one of the directors. The Company Secretary was John Thomas Issott. In the early years senior citizens could attend the Saturday matinee free of charge. It closed in around 1967 and was demolished. A supermarket now stands on the site.

The New Cinema, South Kirkby was opened on (or about) the 2 September 1923 by the South Kirkby Cinema Company Ltd. It seated a mere 350. Cinemascope was fitted in 1957. It closed on 29 May 1982, subsequently becoming a bingo hall. It then became a nightclub but was destroyed by fire in 1991.

four

Pontefract, Ackworth, Streethouse, Featherstone, Purston, Knottingley and Upton

BY HIS MAJESTY'S SERVANTS,
From the THEATRE-ROYAL, YORK,

New Theatre, Pontefract,

On MONDAY Evening, August 3, 1789, will be presented a New COMEDY, call'd, The

CHILD of NATURE.

(Written by Mrs. INCHBALD.)

Perform'd with universal Applause last Season, at the Theatre-Royal, Covent-Garden.

An OCCASIONAL PROLOGUE, by Mr. CUMMINS.

Marquis Alamanza,	——	Mr	CUMMINS.
Peasant,	——	Mr	FRANKLAND.
Duke Murcia,	——	Mr	MICHELL.
Granada,	——	Mr	DRAYCOTT.
Seville,	——	Mr	WARREN.
Count Valantia,	——	Mr	DARCY.
Marchioness Merida,	——	Mrs	KENNEDY.
Amanthis,	——	Miss	HITCHCOCK.

The EPILOGUE, by Mrs. KENNEDY.

End of the PLAY, a DANCE, call'd The

RURAL LOVERS,

By Mr. and Mrs. LASSELLS.

To which will be added a MUSICAL ENTERTAINMENT, called The

FARMER.

Valentine,	——	Mr	DARCY.
Farmer Blackberry,	——	Mr	MICHELL.
Rundy,	——	Mr	SOUTHGATE.
Colonel Dormant,	——	Mr	WARREN.
Fairly,	——	Mr	DRAYCOTT.
Farmer Stubble,	——	Mr	LENG.
Waiter,	——	Mr	LASSELLS.
Jemmy Jumps,	——	Mr	FAWCETT.
Molly Maybush,	——	Miss	HITCHCOCK.
Louisa,	——	Mrs	SOUTHGATE.
Landlady,	——	Mrs	FRENCH.
Betty Blackberry,	——	Mrs	FAWCETT.

To begin a Quarter before seven o'Clock.

Tickets,—Box 3s. Pit 2s. Gallery 1s. to be had of Mr. Swalwell, at the Theatre.

Nights of Playing, Mondays, Wednesdays, Fridays and Saturdays.
The Theatre will close on Saturday, August 22.

Prior to 1788 Pontefract had a theatre of sorts in Newgate. Tate Wilkinson, the actor-manager who held the York Theatre Circuit, refers in his memoirs, *The Wandering Patentee*, to his company going to Pontefract for the first time in 1779 where, he says, 'They found a little building, called by the inhabitants a Playhouse'. He adds, 'The success they met with, and the genteel neighbouring families who honoured their stage endeavours, gave rise to my ruminating at some time to have a regular theatre built and established there on that little pleasant Montpellier of Yorkshire'. Pontefract's new theatre was erected in Gillygate in 1788-89 by ten shareholders (including one woman). It was stone-built and was leased initially to Wilkinson. From 1790, when Pontefract racecourse was laid out, the company came at the time of the races. In June 1837 the theatre was sold to trustees for a school run by the Wesleyan Methodists. The playbill is for the first night at the newly built theatre.

Right: Pontefract's Assembly rooms are a part of the Town Hall complex. Films were shown there on an ad hoc basis from at least as early as 1900 when Pontefract Liberal Association put them on. In September 1912, no doubt hoping to cash in on the growing market for cinema entertainment, Pontefract's councillors decided to seek a tenant who would, for a trial period of two years, use the Assembly Rooms for moving pictures. One Mr Daly took up the offer. In December the town's Surveyor was ordered to install a projection box.

Below: The interior of the Assembly rooms.

The photograph advertising the pantomime at the Assembly Rooms dates from about 1920.

Right: The Assembly rooms were for many years the regular venue for Pontefract Amateur Operatic Society. The Society was founded in 1928 but went into abeyance during the Second World War. Its first production after the war was *The Mikado* in 1949 and was in the Assembly Rooms. The Society came to an end in 2002.

Below: The Turk's Head was licensed for the showing of films from 1910 to 1912. The licensee was George Bassindale.

PONTEFRACT AMATEUR OPERATIC SOCIETY

Affiliated to The National Operatic & Dramatic Association

present

" THE GEISHA "

(by permission of Emile Littler)

Music by : SIDNEY JONES   Book by : OWEN HALL

Lyrics by : HARRY GREENBANK

The entire production by

FRANK HOPKINSON

Director of Music   -   -   Eric A. Holden, F.R C.O.

Scenery by -   Messrs. Dobsworth and Spencer, Bradford

Costumes by   -   -   Chas. H. Fox, Ltd., London
                                 Fashion Hire Ltd., London

IN

THE ASSEMBLY ROOMS, PONTEFRACT

MONDAY to SATURDAY,

APRIL 26th to MAY 1st, 1954

AT 7-15 P.M.   DOORS OPEN 6.30 P.M.

Printed by J. Atkinson & Sons, Star Works, Pontefract.   Tel. 363.

Pontefract's first 'modern' theatre, the Alexandra, was built in Front Street, Tanshelf, in 1906–8 for
Selina Ann Driver. The architects were Garside and Pennington. It opened on 7 July 1908. Quite

EFRACT

15

soon after its opening it included films in its programme: in March 1909, for example, patrons saw a film of the Grand National. After Mrs Driver's death in 1926 it was sold at auction.

Above: The Alexandra was converted as a cinema in 1935.

Left: Taken over by the Star Circuit, the Alexandra was one of its first cinemas to be turned over to bingo, in 1961. It was demolished in 1972.

Above: Originally named simply the Picture House, the Premier, in Front Street, Tanshelf, was Pontefract's first purpose-built cinema. It was built by Albert Wilcock on the site of a tannery. One of four sons of the owner of Pontefract saw mill, Wilcock initially followed his father through an apprenticeship as a joiner and then, after his father's premature death, ran the saw mill with his elder brother, Richard. The younger brothers, George and Frederick, later came into the business too. The Picture House opened on 25 March 1912. A contemporary newspaper report described it as having 'three series of seats in the pit and a commodious gallery'.

Right: It was perhaps the novelty of cinema projection, or the technical skill required, that led the proprietor to advertise the name of the 'operator and electrician' (Fred J. Sharpe) in the early newspaper notices. The Premier was bought by T.C. Holden of Pontefract, who also acquired the Hippodrome at Featherstone, and remained an independent cinema until entertainment tax made it uneconomic and it closed on 29 September 1956. The last films were *Yukon Vengeance* and *Magnificent Roughnecks.*

SCHEDULES now on Sale at all the local Stationers.
Price 2d. each.

THE PICTURE HOUSE,
Tanshelf, Pontefract.

Operator and Electrician — Mr. Fred J. Sharpe.

Monday, September 23, and during the Week.
MATINEE on SATURDAY at 2-30, doors open at 2. Admission—1d., 2d., and 3d.; Adults usual prices.

The Programme will include :—
Nellie, the Lion Tamer
Nick Winter and the Banker
Diamond Cut Diamond
A Sioux Lover's Strategy
Sea Gulls
Over the Divide
Torquay and Cockerington
Simple Simon Fights a Duel
Mother's Prayer
Treasure Island
Spider's Web
Tweedledum Insures his Life
Pack of Hounds
Reconstructed Rebel
Picture Idol
How Pat's Eyes were opened
The Latest News in Pictures
Gaumont's Graphic, and others.

DOORS OPEN 7-15 ; COMMENCE 7-45.
SATURDAYS : Two Performances 6-45 and 9-0.
Pictures Changed Mondays and Thursdays.
Prices of Admission—
3d. 4d. 6d. 9d.
Half-price at 9 o'clock to all parts.

LEEDS INDUSTRIAL

Above: The interior of the Playhouse Cinema, Pontefract. Cinema building was interrupted nationally by the Great War. George Hutchinson stole a march by converting the old theatre in Gillygate into a picture house in 1917. It opened as the Picture Playhouse on 5 December 1917. It was served by two Power's No. 6 projectors, built by the American manufacturers, Nicholas Power Company. In the early years of cinema it was usual for only one projector to be installed but as films got longer it became increasingly important to have two so that films could be shown without a break for a change of reel. Hutchinson's son, George, served as the operator and electrician. Hutchinson's enterprise was to an extent initially thwarted. The lack of available labour meant that the new cinema opened with its balcony incomplete and without the planned redecoration. The Picture Playhouse remained an independent cinema, with George taking over from his father in around 1955. It closed in February 1965 after developers gained planning permission to build shops on the site.

Opposite above: The Crescent Cinema opened on 1 November 1926 during the general strike. Built by the Pontefract Cinema Company, it occupied – and still occupies – a prime site in Ropergate. The architects were the local practice of Hustler and Taylor. The style was somewhat eclectic. The foyer was Jacobean, with oak panels. The auditorium, however, which could seat 1,200, was described as 'new Greek'. The cinema had an organ, built by W. Andrews of Bradford. It had 1,389 pipes and 21 tubular bells and had such novelty effects as a steam whistle, a boat whistle and side drums. The first manager was H.J. Wil-de-gose. The Crescent became part of the Star chain in the 1940s. Like all cinemas, it was badly affected by the drop in patrons in the 1960s. After a short period of closure in early 1970, it reopened on 12 July under the name Studio 1 with bingo in the stalls area and a new cinema, seating 450, created from the circle. Projection was effected by means of a giant periscope! Coral Snooker took the lower half of the building in 1984. At much the same time, Cannon Cinemas acquired the Star chain. In 1987 the lease was bought from Cannon by Al and Lilian Brook-Smith. In the 1990 the lease was sold to Garrick House Cinemas and subsequently to Facealpha. In October 1993, Facealpha went into receivership. In 2006 the Crescent housed Breaks Snooker Club.

Queueing for a children's matinee at the Crescent.

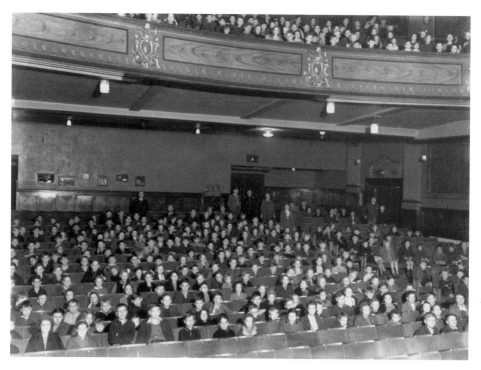

A children's matinee at the Cresent, *c.* 1948.

The Crescent auditorium following a refurbishment.

For a brief period Ackworth had two cinemas. The Alhambra has left little trace. It was first licensed in 1913 and was run by H. Pemberton. The Electric Cinema was simply the upper floor of Ackworth Moor Top Working Men's Club and was licensed from 1915. The pay-box was on the ground floor. The auditorium was a mere 86ft long and 26ft wide. A stage added a further 16ft to the overall length. At one time it had a reed organ. The lessee in 1929, E. Crossley, applied for a stage-play licence explaining that he was losing money on films. The county architect seems to have been quite horrified when he inspected the premises. The cinema floor was of wooden joists and boards, there was no fire-proofing between the ground-floor club and the cinema, the proscenium curtain was neither rigid nor fire-proof and the lavatory accommodation was totally inadequate. The licence was refused. Shortly afterwards the secretary of the Working Men's Club applied for the renewal of the cinema licence but this too was refused. It was the end of moving pictures in Ackworth. Patrons then had the choice of travelling to Wakefield or Pontefract in particular or to other nearby towns and villages.

Above: Streethouse developed as a mining village in the nineteenth century. Its cinema, in Gin Lane, lacked any sort of architectural pretension. The site was bought in 1919 by the West Yorkshire Cinema Company and the cinema was opened by 1921 and was later taken over by the Silverwood family. It served the colliery communities of Streethouse and New Sharlston. It closed in the mid-1950s and serves now as premises for a fencing business.

Below: When Featherstone's first Assembly Rooms were built is not certain but at an auction at the Junction Inn on 1 October 1874, a group of buildings was offered for sale which stood at the junction of Weeland Road and Station Road included shops and dwelling houses with a 'large assembly room' above them. An upper-floor room elsewhere in Featherstone was also used for assemblies and plays with T.J. Sides as its lessee. The West Riding County Council granted Sides' premises a theatre licence in the first years of the twentieth century although normally with some caveat requiring improvements

to be carried out. It may well have been there that Featherstone people first saw moving pictures – in November 1901 Harry Buxton's 'famous operatic choir and cinema performance' was presented at what was, rather ambitiously, advertised as the 'Theatre Royal'. From 1911 to 1913 Sides held a cinema licence for the Featherstone Hotel.

It was not unusual for public swimming baths – themselves a feature of the second half of the nineteenth century – to be boarded over during the winter and used as dance floors or for other entertainment. In the winter of 1910-11 and 1911-12, the Lister Baths in Featherstone became the village's first cinema. On 25 November 1910, Bert Bernard from Wakefield Hippodrome gave 'the first cinematograph exhibition of the season'. For the second season, which opened on 9 October 1911, the baths were hired by Fred Buxton of Douglas. After Buxton opened the Hippodrome in 1912 the baths was advertised as the Kozey Picture House.

The Baths were provided for the people of Featherstone by Hon. John Cunliffe-Lister, the owner of very large collieries in the area. They were opened on 25 May 1910 before a considerable crowd. The ceremony was performed by Roslyn Holiday, the donor's agent.

STATION ROAD, FEATHERSTONE

The formal opening of Featherstone's first cinema, the Palace (towards the right of the picture) was performed by J. Walmsley JP on 23 December 1911, little over a month after building work had commenced! The work was carried out by Heath and Co. of Salford and Manchester for the Manchester-based Electric Theatre Syndicate. According to the contemporary newspaper report, it was built of concrete with an asbestos roof. It had a raked floor and seated 820. The screen was simply the wall at the back of the stage. The proprietors made a virtue of this claiming that, because they had not used a canvas screen, the pictures would be steadier and clearer. It had alternative electric and gas lighting installations, the former provided by its own generators. In its second week it showed a film of the *Delhi Durbar*, a mass assembly outside Delhi to mark the coronation of George V as Emperor of India. The first licence was issued to John Thomas Issott who was to be involved in a number of further cinemas in the Hemsworth area.

Opposite above: The amateur group, the Featherstone Music and Dramatic Society, which was founded in the early 1940s, presented its first productions at the Lister Baths although *The Gondoliers*, performed in 1945, was the last there for some years. Their 1968 pantomime of *Mother Goose* was given at the Baths.

Opposite below: Featherstone Miners' Welfare Hall, the first phase of which was opened in 1898, also provided facilities for variety shows, plays and musicals. The Featherstone amateurs, who had just extended their name to the Featherstone and District Music and Dramatic Society, moved there in 1946 to take advantage of the larger stage. The Welfare Hall is on the right of the picture.

Competition from the Hippodrome must have proved too much for the Palace. In February 1918 the company applied for the third time, but now successfully, for a licence to run it as a billiard hall. At the hearing it was said that Featherstone had nineteen billiard tables but that sixteen of these were in public houses. The company presented a petition with 200 signatures including that of the vicar who supported the application because it would be an alternative to public houses and no gambling would be allowed.

The Hippodrome was built for Fred Buxton and opened with films and variety entertainment on 23 November 1912. It was sold in 1920 to T.C. Holden of Pontefract. In the mid-1960s it began to operate as a bingo hall for three days a week. Its last film, *The Guns of Navarone*, was shown in the second week of September 1966.

Above: Children gathered for a Tom Thumb Club matinee at the Hippodrome in 1931.

Right: In 1952 Featherstone Rovers went to Wembley for the first time for the final of the Rugby League Challenge Cup. The team lost but there were jubilant scenes outside the Hippodrome on the players' return.

Above: Taken in February 2005, the photograph records the last days of Featherstone Hippodrome.

Left: Theatre proprietors in both Castleford and Pontefract sought to draw patrons from Featherstone as these advertisements, placed at the bottom of Station Road (and half concealed by floods) demonstrate. It is thought that photograph was taken in 1922.

The Jubilee Hotel, Featherstone, has been a venue for concerts and variety shows on many occasions.

Purston never had a purpose-built cinema but between 1910 and 1912 the Junction Inn was licensed for the showing of films.

Left: Films were shown at Knottingley Town Hall on a regular basis from 1912 until 1925. In 1912 the licensee was Walter Swaine. The 'cinema' there was shortly afterwards run in conjunction with the Palace with J. Harris as the licensee from 1914 to 1920 and RTA as the licensees from 1920 until 1925.

Opposite below: The Palace in Aire Street was Knottingley's sole purpose-built cinema. It was established by the Knottingley Picture Palace Company Ltd and designed by the Pontefract firm of Penington, Hustler and Taylor. It opened on 25 February 1913. Since the film advertised here, *At the Foot of the Scaffold*, was released in 1913, the cinema may have been quite newly opened when this picture was taken. The Palace was taken over briefly in 1920 by RTA, the company which had built Castleford Picture House. The longest tenancy was that of Donald Wood who took over the lease in 1931 and retained control until selling the business to Star Cinemas (London) Ltd in December 1953. In the years before and after the Second World War, Wood had managed to deter the growing chains from coming to Knottingley by gaining planning permission himself for a second cinema at the junction of Weeland Road and Spawd Bone Lane. In the event it was never built. The Palace closed on 3 December 1960.

Above: The paybox at the Palace Cinema, taken during an archaeological survey in 2002 prior to its conversion into dwellings.

Right: The Palace Cinema following its conversion to residential accommodation.

REGENT

UPTON.   **CINEMA**   **PHONE 237**

Proprietors: Managing Director: Circuit Manager: Resident Manager:
REGENT (Upton) LTD.   WALTER ECKART   STEVE ROBERTS   ROBERT K. BULLEYMENT

WEEK COMMENCING MONDAY, DEC. 27TH, 1948

MONDAY 5-30 & 8-10 P.M.   TUESDAY 6-30 P.M.

CHESTER MORRIS & LLOYD NOLAN in

COUNTERFEIT

Ⓐ IT'S TOUGH!   IT'S TREMENDOUS!

RUDY VALEE in TIME OUT FOR RHYTHM

WEDNESDAY 5-30 & 8-10 P.M.   THURSDAY 6-30 P.M.

GEORGE MURPHY & LUCILLE BALL in

THE NAVY STEPS OUT

Ⓤ FORGET YOUR TROUBLES — SEE THIS GREAT ROMANTIC LAUGH

also STADIUM HIGHLIGHTS

FRIDAY 6-30 P.M.   SATURDAY 5-30 & 8-10 P.M.

SHIRLEY TEMPLE, FRANCHOT TONE, GUY MADISON in

TWO MEN AND A GIRL

THREE STARS—A GREAT CAST—IN A MERRY MATRIMONIAL MIX-UP

ALSO IN CINECOLOUR

ROMANCE OF THE WEST

starring EDDIE DEAN

SATURDAY MORNING DOORS OPEN AT 9-30 P.M.

UPTON YOUNG CITIZENS MATINEE CLUB

ADMISSION 6d.   HAVE YOU JOINED YET   ADMISSION 6d.

BOOKABLE SEATS FOR ALL PERFORMANCES.

To Comply with Regulations the Management regret they are unable to admit Children under 5 or Babies in Arms—All Children Must be Paid For — Special Prices For Children.

TAYLORS. COLOUR PRINTERS. WOMBWELL. YORKS.

Like many other cinemas in the Wakefield District, the Regent at Upton was built to serve a colliery community. In fact the proprietors bought the site, on Wrangbrook Road, from the Colliery Company. Building work, undertaken by the firm of Frank Haslam Ltd, Doncaster, began in January 1934 and the cinema was opened on 11 June 1934 with *Peg o' my Heart*. The commissionaire for some years was Mr Buttle. The children's matinees were run by Uncle Bob, followed by Uncle Peter (Dennis Hurst, who also ran the Plaza at Fitzwilliam). Birthdays were celebrated by the child going onto the stage in front of a screened picture of a birthday cake. Among the Regent's best known patrons was comedian Charlie Williams (1927-2006) who, for a time, lived in Upton and worked at Upton Colliery before he found fame. The Regent was taken over by Star Cinemas in 1937. Patrick Duffy, who was the projectionist there at the time of the closure, remembers that during the war the cinema put on a free show on Sunday mornings for members of the Home Guard. The staff worked on those occasions without wages. After its closure in around 1960 the Regent became a clothing factory. Later it became Hughes's timber yard. It was demolished in the first years of the twenty-first century.

Bibliography

Benton, R., 'Ryhill Cinemas', in *Ryhill in History* Vol. I, Ryhill Parish Council and Wakefield District Council, 1981.

Berry, L.A., and Williams, D.M. (eds), *Featherstone: A Glimpse of the Past*, Countryside Publications, 1986.

Cunniff, Tom, *Battye's Pontefract*, Barracuda Books, 1987.

Eyles, Allen, *ABC, The First Name in Entertainment*, Cinema Theatre Association, 1993.

Featherstone Chronicle, May 1990 and November 1990.

Hornsey, Brian, *Star Cinemas: Britain's leading independent cinema circuit*, Fuchsiaprint, 2005.

Lumb, Tony, *Featherstone: The Millennium Tome*, Briton Press, 2000.

Rose, Martial, *The Wakefield Mystery Plays,* London, 1961.

Smith, *The Cinemas of Mexborough and the Dearne Valley*, Mercia Cinema Society, 1995.

Spencer, Terry, *Palace Cinema, Knottingley*, privately printed, 1999.

Taylor, C.M.P, *Right Royal: Wakefield Theatre 1776-1994*, Wakefield Historical Publications, 1995.

Taylor, C.M.P., *Cinema Story: the rise, fall and renewal of Wakefield Picture Houses*, Mercia Cinema Society, 1996.

Taylor, Kate, *50 Years of the ABC Regal Wakefield*, Wakefield Historical Publications, 1985.

Walker, Brian, (ed) *Frank Matcham, Theatre Architect*, 1980.

Westfield Local History Group, *South Elmsall in the Making*, 1991.

Westfield Local History Group, *South Elmsall: A Family Village*, 1994.

Westfield Local History Group, *South Elmsall Picture Memories*, 2000.

Wilkinson, Tate, *The Wandering Patentee*, 1795.

Williams, C, *Castleford Town Trail*, Wakefield Committee for European Achitectural Heritage Year, 1975.

Other local titles published by Tempus

Wakefield Revisited
PAUL DAWSON

Straddling the border between the wool and textile towns to the west and the coal mining villages to the south and east, Wakefield rose to national prominence in 1889 as the county town of the West Riding of Yorkshire. This collection of more than 200 images, spanning the last two centuries and separated into sections such as City Scenes, Georgian Housing, Churches and Chapels, La Garde Imperiale and Wakefield at War, will delight newcomers and residents alike.

0 7524 2491 2

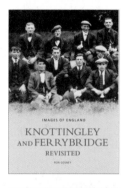

Knottingley and Ferrybridge Revisited
RON GOSNEY

Knottingley and Ferrybridge have changed considerably over the last 100 years. Many older buildings, especially in Aire Street, Knottingley and The Square, Ferrybridge, were demolished as the pottery and shipbuilding industries which had formerly dominated the area fell into decline. This fascinating collection of old photographs takes a nostalgic look back, recalling the industry and the people, the churches and the events of the last century.

0 7524 3954 5

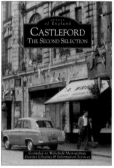

Castleford: The Second Selection
WAKEFIELD METROPOLITAN DISTRICT LIBRARIES AND INFORMATION SERVICES

From glassworks and potteries to flour mills, boat-building and of course the collieries, the town and its people are seen at work – and at play – in the town's various bands, sports teams and special events, including the 'Reight Neet Aht'. Containing more than 200 archive images, *Castleford: The Second Selection* will delight all those who know and love the area.

0 7524 1563 8

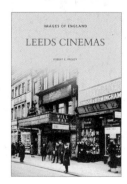

Leeds Cinemas
ROBERT E. PREEDY

Through the medium of old photographs, programmes and advertisements, this book provides a fascinating look at the history of cinema-going in the city of Leeds and its suburbs over the last hundred years. Including chapters on technology, entrepreneurs and cinema chains, *Leeds Cinemas* will delight all those who have fond memories of visiting some of Leeds' picture houses, many of which have now disappeared, as well as anyone interested in the architectural and social history of the city.

0 7524 3583 1

If you are interested in purchasing other books published by Tempus, or in case you have difficulty finding any Tempus books in your local bookshop, you can also place orders directly through our website

www.tempus-publishing.com